French: Short Stories for Intermediate Level + AUDIO

Improve your French listening comprehension skills with seven French stories for intermediate level

"Best blog dedicated to the French Language and Culture for 2014, 2015, and 2016."
(Voted by the Language Portal blab.la and its community)

Other books in this series:

Learn French With Stories: 7 Short Stories For Intermediate Students Vol. 2

Also available:

Learn French with Stories for Beginners Vol. 1
Learn French with Stories for Beginners Vol. 2
Learn French with Stories for Beginners Vol. 3

For more products by Frédéric BIBARD/Talk in French, visit
https://www.amazon.com/Frederic-BIBARD (for US)
https://www.amazon.co.uk/Frederic-BIBARD (for UK)
or go to
https://store.talkinfrench.com.

INTRODUCTION

Learn French in a more natural and entertaining way.

How does a child learn to talk, speak and read? By experience! Someone who cares talks to them, reads to them and teaches them how to write. What little child doesn't like to have a story read to them? Learn how to communicate in French the same way. It doesn't have to be complicated to be effective and enjoyable.

This book contains 7 original French short stories designed to help you **improve your reading and listening skills** and **learn new vocabulary easily.** The stories are fun and engaging. They are written for beginner to low intermediate French learners [or A2 level on the Common European Framework of Reference (CEFR)].

Enjoy yourself while you learn to speak French.

A common complaint for those learning to speak French is how difficult it is to find suitable reading material, and the lack of audio content to practice listening and pronunciation. This book provides a solution for both of those problems. It gives the reader a fun way to learn how to read, speak, listen to and pronounce French without getting bored or intimidated by the monotony of memorizing grammar rules and vocabulary lists. Have fun while learning French!

Useful story themes cultivate a natural development to speaking French instinctively.

Imagine listening to your favorite story. Learning happens naturally. Here, your brain puts the pieces of vocabulary and grammar structures together as you spend time in stories that revolve around real life scenarios. Then, use what you learn in your day-to-day conversations. You retain more because you can actually use it! In learning this way, your instincts connected with communication are engaged and your conversation will flow naturally.

Also, this format makes it easy for you to do away with the dictionary! (Thank heavens.) French-English glossaries are tucked into the stories to help you understand certain words. Not only will you will be introduced to over 700 new French words and expressions, but you will learn how to use them in the proper context.

Boost your progress by using the summary exercises at the end of each story to practice your writing skills.

The stories are not only interesting to read but also revolve around **useful situations.** You learn about: travelling, love, relationships, cooking, shopping, school, movies

Advice on how to use this book effectively

While you can choose your own way of enjoying this book, I have prepared some advice on how you can take full advantage of it and maximize your learning and enjoyment.

1. **Don't try to understand everything the first time around.** As a beginner, your French skills will take time to develop. You may not understand everything. That's OK. Don't give up or get frustrated just because you are stuck on one word. I have tried to provide as much vocabulary as possible that I believe can instill in your mind the comprehension of the stories. If one word confuses you, just skip it and continue reading.

2. **Beware of direct translation.** You may have already learned some individual French words separately. Sometimes, though, when these words are put together, the meaning completely changes. Be careful not to translate word for

word. For example: « tout le monde » (literal meaning « all the world ») = everybody. The same idea applies for phrasal verbs. For example: « se mettre » (literal meaning « to put yourself ») = to start / to begin.

3. **Make use of the summary**. Each story comes with a sample summary. After reading each story, I encourage you to write your own summary to reinforce the learning process. After creating a summary based on your comprehension, compare it with the one provided. I highly recommend completing this exercise. It's a good way to boost your writing skills.

4. **Review the words you learned.** The vocabulary recap at the end of each chapter allows a review which will help you recall and retain the new vocabulary and expressions you learned in the story.

Improve your listening and pronunciation skills with the audio recording

Your book comes with the audio recording of each story, narrated by a native French speaker. Your comprehension of the spoken word will increase as your ears hear how the words sound and when you practice the pronunciation out loud while listening. The simple way a child learns how to communicate is the same method used here: practice and experience.

The stories are recorded in two ways:

- A slow version helps beginners improve their pronunciation
- A normal and natural speed furthers the intermediate and advanced learners' listening and comprehension skills

For beginner-level learners:

1. Read through the story first, focusing on understanding its subject matter and learning the vocabulary.

2. Then listen to the slow audio version to practice your listening comprehension and pronunciation.

3. Now listen to the natural speed version, increasing your ability to understand the story at this speed.

For intermediate to advanced-level learners:

1. Listen to the stories first. Confirm your understanding of them by reading it and checking out the vocabulary.

2. If you need to review, read the story, decide where your understanding needs improvement and start there!

How can you download the audio?

On the last page of this e-book, you will find the link which enables you to download the MP3 files that accompany this book. Save the files onto any device and listen to the stories anywhere.

Want hands free?

If you would like a hands free and purely audible way to learn French, check out the book on Audible. It provides you with the stories, meanings, vocabulary, the French/English glossary...all of it...**and more** - all audibly.

Instead of over two hours of story-telling, you receive more than 17 hours of audio. Needs hands free in the car, while you exercise or shop? This is the answer. Anywhere you go, whatever you're doing, your Audible version of the book goes with you.

For those of you without an Audible account, you can get this book **for free with Audible's 30-Day Trial.** You can unsubscribe any time and the book remains yours. To get the audiobook version for free, go to amazon and plug "audible" in the search box. Click on the "audible" icon and choose "Try Audible." You will be directed to the trial offer. Follow the steps provided to get your free book! (Should you enjoy your audible account, the $14.95/month renewal is automatic.)

Want hands free?

To get "Spanish Short Stories for Beginners" for **free**

1) Go here http://bit.ly/french-intermediate for **amazon.com**

Or here **for Amazon UK**

http://bit.ly/french-intermediate-uk

2/ Click (or tap) on **Try Audible for FREE**

3/ Follow the remaining steps, and that's it.

Table of Contents

Histoire 1/ Story 1:
Les Dubois partent en vacances

Important! The link to download the MP3 is available at the end of this book (page 133).

En rentrant du travail, M. Dubois se demandait où il allait **emmener** sa famille en vacances. Les enfants ayant fini leurs **années scolaires** et sa période de **congé toute proche**, M. Dubois voulait **faire plaisir** à **tout le monde** en les emmenant visiter un nouveau pays pour les vacances.

Emmener - ***to drive/to take***
Années scolaires - ***school years/academic years***
Congé - ***vacation/holiday***

Histoire 1/ Story 1: Les Dubois partent en vacances

Toute proche - ***approaching***
Faire plaisir à tout le monde - ***to make everyone happy***
Tout le monde - ***everyone***

Une fois à la maison, M. Dubois parle à sa femme de son projet de vacances:

"Chérie, **j'ai vraiment envie** d'aller à l'étranger cette fois-ci pour les vacances."

Mme. Dubois lui répond: "Ah ! Ça c'est une bonne idée! Mais pouvons- **nous nous permettre** des vacances à l'étranger?" Son mari la rassure et lui dit: "**Ne t'en fais pas** pour ça. **Nos économies** peuvent nous faire faire **le tour du monde."**

J'ai vraiment envie - ***I really want***
D'aller- ***go (to go)***
À l'étranger - ***abroad***
Nous permettre - ***(to) allow us***

Ne t'en fais pas - ***don't worry***
Nos économies - ***our savings***
Faire le tour du monde - ***to travel around the world***

Très contente, Mme Dubois court appeler ses enfants: "Erwan, Valentine, Isabelle, venez vite, nous avons une surprise pour vous!" Les enfants, **au courant**, ne **cachent** pas leur joie et un conseil de famille est rapidement **mis en place** pour choisir **le lieu** où la famille passera ses vacances.

Au courant - ***aware***
Cachent (cacher) - ***hide (to hide)***
Conseil de famille - ***family meeting***
Mis en place (mettre en place) - ***put in place (to put in place)***
Le lieu - ***the place***

M. Dubois donne à tout le monde **le droit de proposer** sa destination préférée, lui et Mme Dubois ont tous deux proposé le lieu où ils avaient passé leur **lune de miel**, il y a des années de cela. Erwan n'a pas tardé à montrer son refus: "Non! Pas le Brésil (!) Ce n'est plus aussi **sûr** qu'à votre époque, de plus ce n'est pas la période du carnaval de Rio. Si ce n'est que pour aller à la plage **autant rester** en France!" Et il a continué son discours en proposant le Royaume-Uni, ce qui lui **offrirait l'occasion** de revoir ses amis, qu'il avait **connus** lors d'un échange scolaire.

Le droit - ***the right***
Proposer - ***to suggest***
Lune de miel - ***honeymoon***
Sûr – ***safe/secure***
Autant - ***as well (it is probably best to)***
Rester - ***to stay***
Offrirait(offrir) - ***would offer (to offer)***
L'occasion - ***the chance/the opportunity***
Avait connu - ***had known/had met***
Échange scolaire - ***student exchange***

Valentine, elle, **n'était pas de l'avis de** son frère et dit à ses parents: "Papa! Maman! Ne l'**écoutez** pas. Il ne pense qu'à lui. Il refuse le Brésil de vos **souvenirs** en préférant aller voir ses copains. Moi, je vous propose d'aller en Thaïlande: un **dépaysement** total à la rencontre d'une culture exotique tout en **profitant** du soleil."

N'était pas de l'avis de - ***was not of the same opinion as***
L'écoutez (écouter) - ***listen to him (to listen)***
Souvenirs - ***memories***
Dépaysement - ***change of scenery***
En profitant - ***while enjoying***

Isabelle, qui vient à peine de fêter ses treize ans, est d'accord avec sa sœur pour le continent mais pas pour la destination: "Val ! Tuas vraiment raison, l'Asie c'est trop cool. Mais je préférerais aller au Japon. Il y a tellement plus à voir **là-bas.**" M. Dubois se trouve dans une situation **peu réjouissante**. La famille n'arrive pas vraiment à se mettre d'accord sur la destination des vacances.

Histoire 1/ Story 1: Les Dubois partent en vacances

Qui vient à peine de - ***barely/has just turned (13 years old)***
Fêter - ***to celebrate***
Là-bas - ***over there***
Peu réjouissante - ***bleak***

"Nous pouvons **tirer** les destinations **au sort** (= tirer au sort)!" déclare Erwan. Son père lui répond qu'ils ne peuvent pas laisser **le sort** décider de leurs vacances. A ce moment-là, **une sage** idée **traverse l'esprit** de Mme. Dubois qui en parle à son mari: "-Joël ! Pourquoi ne pas **prendre** les quatre destinations **en compte**?!"

Tirer au sort - ***draw lots (pick randomly)***
Sage - ***wise***
Traverse l'esprit - ***crosses the mind***

Prendre en compte - ***to take into account/to consider*** « Tu veux aller visiter quatre pays?!

- Mais bien sûr que non. Prenons un ordinateur et vérifions laquelle parmi les quatre destinations nous **convient** le mieux en matière d'argent, de conditions et de loisirs.
- Très bonne idée Magalie. »

Aller - ***to go***
Ordinateur - ***computer***
Convient (convenir) - ***is suitable (to be suitable)***

Toute la famille **se presse devant** l'ordinateur et après quelque petites recherches il **s'avère que** la Thaïlande est le meilleur choix. "Va pour la Thaïlande!" Annonce M. Dubois. Et il s'occupe de contacter une agence de voyage pour tout organiser.

Se presse (se presser) - ***hurries (to hurry)***
Devant - ***in front of***
Il s''avère que (s'avérer que) - ***it turns out (to turn out)***

Dix jours plus tard, la famille Dubois, **prête à partir,** est en train de **charger** les derniers bagages dans la voiture: "Nous ne **déménageons** pas Valentine! Tu peux laisser quelques **affaires** à la maison."

Prête à partir - ***ready to leave***
Charger - ***to load***
En train de charger - ***in the middle of loading***
Déménageons (déménager) - ***move out (to move out) (house)***
Affaires - ***belongings***

« Mais je prends le **strict nécessaire** Papa ! Dans un voyage comme celui-ci, nous devons être **prêts** à n'importe quelle situation.

– Tu as sûrement raison. **Mais en quoi** une valise pleine de **maillots de bain est- elle nécessaire?** Deux ou trois te suffiront largement. Remets le reste dans ton armoire. Pas de **surplus inutile.**
– D'accord.

Strict nécessaire - ***bare necessities***
Prêts - ***ready***
Mais en quoi - ***but in what/but for what***
Maillots de bain - ***swimsuits***
Est-elle nécessaire - ***is it needed***
Surplus - ***extra***
Inutile - ***useless***

Tant bien que mal, M. Dubois **arrive à** faire rentrer tout le monde et **l'ensemble** des bagages dans la voiture et démarre pour l'aéroport.

Tant bien que mal - ***somehow***
Arrive à faire rentrer - ***succeeds in putting/adjusting***
L'ensemble - ***the whole of/all***

Une fois à l'aéroport, tout le monde **décharge** la voiture avant même que M. Dubois n'aille **garer** la voiture dans le parking de l'aéroport. Il propose à la famille de l'**attendre** devant le comptoir d´enregistrement. Un petit quart d'heure **plus tard,** le père arrive et **s'occupe** des **préparatifs** du vol avec Erwan pendant que tout le reste de la famille **patiente.**

Histoire 1/ Story 1: Les Dubois partent en vacances

Une fois - ***once***
Àl'aéroport - ***at the airport***
Décharge (décharger) - ***unloads (to unload)***
Garer - ***to park***
Attendre - ***to wait***
Plus tard - ***later***
S'occupe (s'occuper) - ***takes care of (to take care of)***
Préparatifs -***preparations***
Patiente - ***waits patiently***

Après une demieheure d'attente, le message **d'embarquement** pour le **vol** Paris-Bangkok retentit, les Dubois se pressent d'aller **se présenter à** la salle d'embarquement puis vers l'avion. Et c'est ainsi que l'aventure Thaïlandaise de la famille Dubois a commencé.

Embarquement - ***departure***
Vol - ***flight***
Se présenter à - ***to show up at***

Douze heures plus tard, les Dubois sont à Bangkok après avoir **tout réglé** avec les **douanes locales.** Ils sortent de l'aéroport où ils sont surpris par deux personnes **brandissant** un drapeau français et une **pancarte** avec Dubois écrit dessus. Isabelle **interpelle** ses parents en disant: "Qui sont ces gens?!" Sa mère lui répond: "Ton père **a tout prévu** depuis la maison. Ce sont très certainement nos guides."

Tout réglé - ***all set***
Douanes locales - ***local customs***
Brandissant (brandisser) – ***brandishing/waving (to brandish/to wave)***
Pancarte - ***sign***
Interpelle (interpeller) - ***shouts out to (to shout out to)***
A tout prévu - ***planned everything***

La famille se dirige vers les guides.Le premier, un Européen assez grand, de grands yeux clairs, et des cheveux noirs,qui ne laissent pas indifférent Valentine, s'avance et se présente: "Bonjour les Dubois!

Bienvenue en Thaïlande. Mon nom est Sébastien je serai l'un de vos guides. Je suis français et je vis en Thaïlande depuis un certain temps déjà."

Le deuxième guide, une locale, s'avance et se présente à son tour: "Bienvenue à Bangkok. Je m'appelle Mani je suis Thaïlandaise. Je serai votre second guide. Vous passerez un très bon **séjour** avec nous." Et les Dubois sont invités à monter dans un petit van garé juste **derrière** les guides qui vont les mener à leur hôtel.

Séjour - ***stay***
Derrière - ***behind***
Les mener à - ***will lead them to (to lead to)***
En chemin Sébastien **s'entretient** avec M. Dubois:

"Vous voulez qu'on vous conduise vers l´un de nos hôtels partenaires ? Vous pouvez **avoir confiance**. Nous travaillons avec eux depuis longtemps et ce sont des gens très sérieux.

- Non je vous **remercie**. J'ai déjà réservé deux chambres à l'hôtel Hansar Bangkok.
- Très bon choix. C'est aussi un de nos partenaires."

S'entretient (s'entretenir)- ***is talking/is having a conversation (to talk/to have a conversation)***
Avoir confiance - ***to trust***
Je vous remercie - ***thank you***

Arrivés à l'hôtel, Mani **s'occupe d'aller** chercher **les clefs** des chambres des Dubois pendant que Sébastien aide Erwan à **descendre** les bagages du van. Une fois dans l'hôtel la famille **s'étonne** de la **beauté** de celui-ci. Pendant que Mani revient avec un **bagagiste** qui conduit les Dubois à leurs chambres, Mani et Sébastien prennent **congé,** laissant les Dubois **se reposer** de leur long trajet: "M. Dubois, je vous ai laissé nos numéros **en cas de besoin**. Vous pouvez m'appeler depuis le téléphone de l'hôtel. Sinon, **comme prévu**, nous nous reverrons en soirée." M. Dubois le remercie avant de rejoindre sa chambre.

Histoire 1/ Story 1: Les Dubois partent en vacances

S'occupe de (s'occuper de) - ***takes care of (to take care of)***
Les clefs - ***the keys***
Descendre - ***to unload***
S'étonne (s'étonner) ***- is surprised (to be surprised)***
Beauté - ***beauty***
Bagagiste - ***porter***
Prendre congé - ***to leave***
Se reposer - ***to take a rest/to rest***
En cas de besoin - ***if necessary***
Comme prévu - ***according to plan***

La soirée arrivée et les Dubois remis de leur long voyage, Mani et Sébastien **reviennent** pour les emmener **dîner** et passer une **merveilleuse** première soirée à Bangkok.

Reviennent (revenir) - ***come back (to come back)***
Dîner – **to have *dinner***
Merveilleuse - ***wonderful/marvelous***

"Bonsoir les Dubois. Alors, **bien remis**?" Lance Sébastien en arrivant. Erwan réplique avec un air étourdi: "Pas trop je sens que mon dos est **en compote**." Le guide lui **sourit** et lui dit: "Le programme de ce soir vient au bon moment à ce que je vois! Après le repas, je vous ai réservé un massage thaï pour bien vous **détendre** après un aussi long voyage." Tout le monde **approuve** avec un grand enthousiasme.

Bien remis - ***well-recovered***
Étourdis - ***dazed***
Mon dos est en compote - ***my back is killing me/sore back***
Sourit (sourire) - ***smiles (to smile)***
Se détendre - ***to relax***
Approuve (approuver) - ***agrees with (to agree with)***

Arrivée au restaurant de l'hôtel, Valentine demande à Sébastien si ce n'est pas **coûteux** de manger dans un restaurant aussi luxueux. Le guide lui répond que grâce au partenariat avec son agence de voyage, ils ont droit à certains **privilèges** sur les tarifs . Il lui signale que ceux-ci sont écrits dans le **dépliant** donné pus tôt

Coûteux - ***costly/expensive***
Privilèges - ***advantages/benefits***
Dépliant - ***leaflet/pamphlet***

Très contente, Valentine **commence à** réfléchir à la suite du voyage. Mani montre que la famille peut avoir un menu exotique et très **raffiné** pour seulement 20 € tout compris. Après un bon repas et un massage très relaxant, la famille repart se reposer pour la nuit.

Commence à (commencer à) - ***is starting to (to start to)***
Raffiné - ***refined***

Quelques jours plus tard et après avoir vu bon nombre d'endroits **incontournables** de la ville, la **gent féminine** de la famille veut aller **faire les magasins** tandis que les hommes préfèrent aller voir le palais royal de Bangkok. N'arrivant pas à se décider, Sébastien et Mani **proposent** de se séparer. Ainsi, chacun fera ce qu'il voudra: l'équipe de Mani fera les magasins et l'équipe de Sébastien ira au palais royal. Les Dubois trouvent que c'est la meilleure des solutions.

Incontournables - ***unavoidable***
Gent féminine - ***womankind***
Faire les magasins - ***to go shopping***
Proposent (proposer) - ***offer (to offer)***

Et c'est parti pour **une sortie** à Bangkok ! L'équipe de Mani se dirige vers un **marché** très **réputé** chez les touristes avec des prix très **attrayants**. Valentine arrive devant un joli paréo qui irait bien avec un de ses maillots de bain, elle désire l'acheter. Elle attrape Mani pour faire la transaction: “Mani vous pouvez m'aider s'il-vous-plaît? J'aimerais acheter ça.”

Et c'est parti - ***here we go***
Une sortie - ***outing***
Marché - ***market***
Réputé - ***renowned***
Attrayants - ***attractive***

« Oui bien sûr. Le vendeur dit qu'il est à 30 Bats. As-tu de la **devise** thaïlandaise sur toi?

– -Oui Papa m'en a donnée. Demande-lui si j'ai droit à une **réduction** si j'en prends deux? Isabelle en veut un elle aussi.
– -Il accepte de te vendre les deux à 50 Bats et c'est son dernier prix, ça te convient?
– -Oui ça me va. »

Devise - ***currency***
Réduction - ***discount***
Ça te convient? - ***does it suit you?***

Valentine, **aux anges** après quelques **achats,** dit à Mani qu'elle, sa sœur et sa mère voudraient bien manger quelque chose. Mani lui dit qu'ici il n'y a que de la **nourriture saine**, délicieuse et pas chère. Les filles **acceptent de tenter** l'expérience et se dirigent vers un vendeur **ambulant** qui vend des **grillades.**

Aux anges (être aux anges) - ***on cloud nine (to be on cloud nine)***
Achats - ***purchases***
Nourriture saine - ***healthy food***
Acceptent de tenter - ***accept to attempt***
Ambulant - ***itinerant (traveling seller)***
Grillades - ***grilled food***

De leur côté, les hommes de la famille, eux, sont **en pleine** expérience culturelle avec un Sébastien très **connaisseur** de l'histoire des lieux. Erwan, quant à lui, est **ravi de l'affaire** qu'il a faite en achetant trois tickets pour le prix de deux. La visite du palais terminée, il reste beaucoup de temps aux Dubois. Ils décident de **se retrouver** et de faire des activités **ensemble**. Dans l'après-midi, ils vont visiter des temples et acheter des **souvenirs**.

En pleine - ***right in the middle***
Connaisseur – ***expert/connoisseur***
Ravi de l'affaire ***delighted by the deal***
Se retrouver - ***to meet up***

Ensemble - ***together***
Souvenirs - ***souvenirs***

Le soir-même, Sébastien et Mani annoncent que leur temps à Bangkok est **terminé** et qu'ils doivent se préparer pour aller à Phuket pour **profiter de** la mer le lendemain. Valentine, toute contente d'avoir l'occasion de mettre ses maillots de bain et son tout nouveau paréo, pose une question à Sébastien: "Vous viendrez avec nous j'espère?"

Sébastien lui répond : "Oui évidemment, nous serons vos guides **tout au long de** votre séjour.

– Ah! Très bien ça me rassure."

Terminé - ***is over/ended***
Profiter de - ***to make the most of/take advantage of/enjoy***
Tout au long de - ***throughout***
Ça me rassure - ***it reassures me***

Le lendemain, les Dubois sont attendus aux portes de leur hôtel par leurs guides qui viennent les chercher avec le même van. Mme Dubois demande: "Combien de temps durera le voyage, Mani ?

– Toute une journée Madame. Nous y allons en van comme ça vous pourrez voir un peu du pays."

Le voyage commence et les paysages **défilent. Ces vues** merveilleuses depuis le van font **oublier** le long voyage aux Dubois qui apprécient le spectacle. Arrivée à Phuket, la famille est **conduite** dans un autre hôtel qui n'est pas **partenaire** de l'agence, ce qui **supprime** les privilèges et les réductions qu'il y avait à Bangkok. Mais le personnel de cet hôtel est bien plus **accueillant** que celui du précédent, qui vient accueillir ses touristes à la porte. La soirée se finit rapidement. Tout le monde pense plus à dormir qu'à autre chose.

Défilent (défiler) - ***pass/scroll (to pass/to scroll)***
Ces vues - ***these views***
Oublier - ***to forget***

Histoire 1/ Story 1: Les Dubois partent en vacances

Conduite - ***driven***
Partenaire - ***partner***
Supprime (supprimer) – ***removes/cancels (to remove/to cancel)***
Accueillant - ***welcoming***

Le lendemain matin, la famille est surprise de voir que l'hôtel où ils sont **logés** possède un sauna et une piscine et est en plus situé tout près de la plage : ce qui laisse un choix énorme **en matière de divertissements.** La famille **s'amuse** énormément durant son séjour à Phuket, mais **hélas**, tout à une fin.Et après quelques jours les Dubois **se dirigent** vers l'aéroport pour repartir en France. Le **cœur lourd** mais **riche en souvenirs,** les Dubois disent au revoir à la Thaïlande.

Logés **–** ***lodged/accommodated***
Énorme - ***huge***
Divertissements - ***entertainment***
S'amuse (s'amuser) - ***has fun (to have fun)***
Hélas - ***unfortunately/sadly***
Se dirigent vers (se diriger vers) **-** ***are headed to (to head to)***
Cœur lourd - ***heavy heart***
Riche en souvenirs - ***rich in memories/full of memories***

Vocabulary Recap 1:

Emmener - ***to drive/to take***
Années scolaires - ***school years/academic years***
Congé - ***vacation/holiday***
Toute proche - ***approaching***
Faire plaisir à tout le monde - ***to make everyone happy***
Tout le monde - ***everyone***
J'ai vraiment envie - ***I really want***
Aaller - ***to go***
À l'étranger - ***abroad***
Nous permettre - ***to allow us***
Ne t'en fais pas - ***don't worry***
Nos économies - ***our savings***
Faire le tour du monde - ***to travel around the world***
Au courant - ***aware***
Cachent (cacher) - ***hide (to hide)***
Conseil de famille - ***family meeting***
Mis en place (mettre en place) - ***put in place (to put in place)***
Le lieu - ***the place***
Le droit - ***the right***
Proposer - ***to suggest***
Lune de miel - ***honeymoon***
Sûr – ***safe/secure***
Autant - ***as well (it is probably best to)***
Rester - ***to stay***
Offrirait(offrir) - ***would offer (to offer)***
L'occasion - ***the chance/the opportunity***
Avait connu - ***had known/had met***
Échange scolaire - ***student exchange***
N'était pas de l'avis de - ***was not of the same opinion as***
L'écoutez (écouter) - ***listen to him***
Souvenirs - ***memories***
Dépaysement - ***change of scenery***
En profitant - ***while enjoying***
Qui venait à peine de - ***barely/has just turned (13 years old)***
Fêter - ***to celebrate***
Là-bas - ***over there***

Histoire 1/ Story 1: Les Dubois partent en vacances

Peu réjouissante - ***bleak***
Tirer au sort - ***draw lots (pick randomly)***
Sage - ***wise***
Traverse l'esprit - ***crosses the mind***
Prendre en compte - ***to take into account/to consider***
Aille (aller) - ***go (to go)***
Ordinateur - ***computer***
Convient (convenir) - ***is suitable (to be suitable)***
Se presse (se presser) - ***hurries (to hurry)***
Devant - ***in front of***
Il s'avère que (s'avérer que) - ***turns out (to turn out)***
Prête à partir - ***ready to leave***
Charger - ***to load***
En train de charger - ***in the middle of loading***
Déménageons(déménager) - ***move out (to move out) (house)***
Affaires - ***belongings***Strict nécessaire - ***bare necessities***
Prêts - ***ready***
Mais en quoi - ***but in what/but for what***
Maillots de bain - ***swimsuits***
Est-elle nécessaire - ***is it needed***
Surplus - ***extra***
Inutile - ***useless***
Tant bien que mal -***somehow***
Arrive à faire rentrer - ***succeeds in putting/adjusting***
L'ensemble - ***the whole of/all***
Une fois - ***once***
À l'aéroport - ***at the airport***
Décharge (décharger) - ***unloads (to unload)***
Garer - ***to park***
Attendre - ***to wait***
Plus tard - ***later***
S'occupe (s'occuper) - ***takes care of (to take care of)***
Préparatifs -***preparations***
Patiente - ***waits patiently***
Embarquement - ***departure***
Vol - ***flight***
Se présenter à - ***to show up at***
Tout réglé (régler) - ***all set***

Histoire 1/ Story 1: Les Dubois partent en vacances

Douanes locales - ***local customs***
Brandissant (brandisser) – ***brandishing/waving (to brandish/to wave)***
Pancarte - ***sign***
Interpelle (interpeller) - ***shouts out to (to shout out to)***
A tout prévu - ***planned everything***
Séjour - ***stay***
Derrière - ***behind***
Les mener à - ***will lead them to (to lead to)***
S'entretient (s'entretenir)- ***is talking/is having a conversation (to talk/to have a conversation)***
Avoir confiance - ***to trust***
Je vous remercie - ***thank you***
S'occupe de (s'occuper de) - ***takes care of (to take care of)***
Les clefs - ***the keys***
À descendre - ***unload***
S'étonne ***- is surprised***
Beauté - ***beauty***
Bagagiste - ***porter***
Prendre congé - ***to leave***
Se reposer - ***to take a rest/to rest***
En cas de besoin - ***if necessary***
Comme prévu - ***according to plan***
Reviennent (revenir) - ***come back (to come back)***
Dîner – ***to have dinner***
Merveilleuse - ***wonderful/marvelous***
Bien remis - ***well-recovered***
Étourdis - ***dazed***
Mon dos est en compote - ***my back is killing me/sore back***
Sourit (sourire) - ***smiles (to smile)***
Se détendre - ***to relax***
Approuve (approuver) - ***agrees with (to agree with)***
Coûteux - ***costly/expensive***
Privilèges - ***advantages/benefits***
Dépliant - ***leaflet/pamphlet***
Commence à (commencer à) - ***is starting to (to start to)***
Raffiné - ***refined***
Incontournables - ***unavoidable***

Histoire 1/ Story 1: Les Dubois partent en vacances

Gent féminine - ***womankind***
Faire les magasins - ***to go shopping***
Proposent (proposer) - ***offer (to offer)***
Et c'est parti - ***here we go***
Une sortie - ***outing***
Marché - ***market***
Réputé - ***renowned***
Attrayants - ***attractive***
Devise - ***currency***
Reduction - ***discount***
Ça te convient? - ***does it suit you?***
Aux anges (être aux anges) ***on cloud nine (to be on cloud nine)***
Achats ***purchases***
Nourriture saine - ***healthy food***
Acceptent de tenter - ***accept to attempt***
Ambulant – ***itinerant (traveling seller)***
Grillades - ***grilled food***
En pleine - ***right in the middle***
Connaisseur – ***expert/connoisseur***
Ravi de l'affaire ***delighted by the deal***
Se retrouver - ***to meet up***
Ensemble - ***together***
Souvenirs - ***souvenirs***
Terminé - ***is over/ended***
Profiter de - ***to make the most of/to take advantage of/to enjoy***
Tout au long de - ***throughout***
Ça me rassure - ***it reassures me***
Défilent (défiler) - ***pass/scroll (to pass/to scroll)***
Des vues - ***these views***
Oublier - ***to forget***
Conduite - ***driven***
Partenaire - ***partner***
Supprime (supprimer) – ***removes/cancels (to remove/to cancel)***
Accueillant - ***welcoming***

Histoire 1/ Story 1: Les Dubois partent en vacances

Logés – ***lodged/accommodated***
Énorme - ***huge***
Divertissements - ***entertainment***
S'amuse (s'amuser) - ***has fun (to have fun)***
Hélas - ***unfortunately/sadly***
Se dirigent vers (se diriger vers) - ***are headed to (to head to)***
Cœur lourd - ***heavy heart***
Riche en souvenirs - ***rich in memories/full of memories***

Practice your writing

Write a short summary of this story.

Sample:

Profitant de quelques semaines de congé et des vacances de ses enfants, M. Dubois décide de prendre toute sa famille à l'étranger pour les vacances. Il est ravi d'en parler . Monsieur et Madame Dubois proposent le pays de leur lune de miel comme destination. Leurs enfants, Erwan, Valentine, et Isabelle, proposent une destination chacun, eux aussi. Après de longues discussions, et quelques comparaisons, c'est finalement la Thaïlande.

Dix jours se sont écoulés depuis le choix de la destination des vacances. Les Dubois chargent leurs voitures et partent pour l'aéroport. Ils passent à l'enregistrement. Ils embarquent et leur aventure Thaïlandaise commence.

Arrivée à Bangkok, la famille Dubois est surprise par deux guides qui sont venus les attendre : « Bonjour ! Nous sommes Sébastien, et Mani. Nous sommes vos guides. » M. Dubois ayant tout prévu, les guides sont venus les chercher et les emmener à leur hôtel.

La première soirée prévue est une soirée de relaxation. Les jours suivants, les Dubois ont bien visité la ville et ont vu tous les lieux emblématiques de Bangkok. Un beau matin, les Dubois n'arrivant pas à se décider sur quoi faire, les guides les séparent en deux équipes : Shopping pour les filles et visite du palais royal pour les hommes. Les filles font plein de bonnes affaires, alors qu'Erwan et son père découvrent la culture thaïlandaise. En fin de journée, leurs guides leur annoncent que le lendemain ils quitteront Bangkok pour Phuket. Ils profiteront des plages du pays.

Les Dubois terminent leurs vacances avec beaucoup de bonheur avant que le moment pour repartir vers la France n'arrive. Les Dubois sont tristes. Ils **rembarquent** pour la France, mélancoliques, mais le cœur plein de souvenirs.

Rembarquer - ***to re-embark***

Histoire/Story 2:
Un nouveau lycée

Sa famille ayant **déménagée**, Robin n'a pas eu le choix et a dû changer de **lycée** à la **rentrée** pour un lycée plus **proche** de leur nouvelle maison, ce qui ne l'**enchantait** pas vraiment. Il **redoutait** beaucoup son premier jour dans ce tout nouveau lycée où il ne connaissait personne, premier jour qui n'**a pas tardé** pas à venir.

Histoire/Story 2: Un nouveau lycée

Déménagée **- (déménager)** - *moved house* ***- (to move house)***
Lycée - ***secondary school/high school***
Rentrée - ***start of the school year***
Proche – ***close/near/nearby***
Enchantait **(enchanter)** - *enchanted* ***- (to enchant)***
Redoutait (redouter) - ***feared (to fear)***
A tardé (tarder) – ***took a long time (to take a long time)***

Le matin de la rentrée, Robin **traîne** dans son lit, **voulant** à tout prix retarder ce moment qu'il redoute tant. Sa mère ne **cesse** de l'appeler pour qu'il **se dépêche** de **se préparer** pour venir prendre son petit déjeuner. **Tant bien que mal,** Robin **parvient** à s'habiller et arrive dans la cuisine en demandant à ses parents:

Traîne (traîner) – ***dawdles/lags behind (to dawdle/to lag behind)***
Voulant à tout prix - ***desperate to***
Cesse (cesser) ***- ceases (to cease)***
Se dépêche (se dépêcher) - ***hurries (to hurry)***
Se préparer - ***to get ready***
Tant bien que mal - ***somehow***
Parvient à - ***manages to***

"C'est si **indispensable** que ça l'école?!" Son père lui répond en souriant:

"Ne t'en fais pas ! Ça va très bien se passer. Et tu te feras plein de nouveaux copains.

- Mais j'aurais voulu **rester** dans mon lycée.
- C'est impossible ! Nous avons un lycée dans notre nouveau **quartier**, et ton ancien lycée est trop loin. C'est plus **rassurant** de te savoir proche de la maison."

Indispensable - ***essential***
Rester ***- to stay***
Quartier – ***district/neighborhood***
Rassurant – ***reassuring***

Forcé d'accepter la situation, Robin **avale** rapidement son petit déjeuner et s'en va pour l'école.

Arrivé au lycée, Robin **se fait** vite **remarquer** par le surveillant, qui **s'approche** de lui et lui dit: "Que faites-vous ici? Je ne vous ai jamais vu dans notre lycée." Robin, tout surpris de l'**accueil,** lui répond rapidement:

"Bonjour ! Je m'appelle Robin Fournier. Je viens d'être transféré. J'arrive du Lycée Ronsard.

– Ah! Je vois. **Suivez**-moi."

Avale (avaler)- ***swallows (to swallow)***
Se fait remarquer (se faire remarquer) - ***gets noticed (to get noticed)***
S'approche (s'approcher) - ***gets close (to get close)***
L'accueil - ***the welcome/the reception***
Être transféré – ***to be transferred***
Suivez (suivre) - ***follow (to follow)***

Robin est **conduit** par le surveillant dans les bureaux de l'administration où une dame plus souriante lui dit : « Bienvenue mon petit Robin! J'espère que tu **te plairas** chez nous. Un transfert **au beau milieu de l'année** ce n'est jamais facile. Mais **rassure-toi,** tout le monde sera gentil avec toi.

Conduire - ***to bring/to take somewhere***
Te plairas (se plaire) — ***enjoy yourself (to enjoy oneself)***
Au beau milieu de — ***right in the middle of***
Rassure-toi — ***don't worry***

- D'accord, merci Madame.
- Tu es dans la classe de Mademoiselle Martin. C'est ton **professeur principal**, elle **t'enseignera** la philosophie. Suis-moi. Je te conduis à ta **salle de classe.**
- D'accord, merci beaucoup. »

Histoire/Story 2: Un nouveau lycée

Professeur principal - ***homeroom teacher***
Enseignera (enseigner) - ***will teach (to teach)***
Salle de classe - ***classroom***

En chemin vers sa classe, Robin a l'occasion de **visiter** un peu **les lieux**: bibliothèque, cantine, club de science, club de musique, etc... Robin se dit qu'il y a plus d'**activités extra-scolaires** dans ce nouveau lycée.

En chemin - ***on the road/on the way***
Visiter les lieux - ***visit the premises***
Activités extra-scolaires - ***extra-curricular activities***
Arrivée en face de la salle de classe, la dame **frappe** et ouvre la porte, **en s'adressant** au professeur qui faisait son cours:
Frappe (frapper) - ***knocks (to knock)***
En s'adressant au(à) - ***addressing***

"Excusez-moi ! Mlle. Martin. Je vous amène un tout nouvel élève. Il s'appelle Robin Fournier. Je vous le **confie.**

- \- Oui! Certainement. Bonjour Robin. **Installe-toi,** à coté de Sandrine **au fond**."

Tout intimidé, Robin va vite **prendre place** sans **prononcer** le **moindre mot.** Et le cours se **poursuit** normalement. À la fin de la leçon, Sandrine, la voisine de Robin, lui parle: "Salut ! Moi c'est Sandrine. Qu'est-ce qui t'amène dans notre lycée?

- Mes parents ont acheté une maison un peu plus loin. Ils ont pensé que ça serait mieux que je vienne ici.
- D'accord ! Et tu te plais **dans le coin**?
- Je viens d'arriver donc je n'ai pas **d'avis** trop précis pour le moment.

  - Ok ! Le prochain cours ce sont les maths. **Méfie-toi** du prof, il aime faire passer les nouveaux au **tableau** sans crier gare."

Confie (confier) - ***entrust (to entrust)***
Installe-toi (s'installer) - ***sit (to sit)***
Au fond (de la classe) - ***the back (of the class)***
Prendre place - ***to take a seat***
Prononcer - ***to pronounce/to utter/to say***
Le moindre mot (expression) – ***any/a single word (expression)***
Poursuit (poursuivre) - ***carries on with/continues (to carry on with/ to continue)***
Dans le coin - ***in the neighborhood***
Avis - ***opinion***
Méfie - ***distrust***
Tableau - ***board (blackboard)***

La discussion de Robin et de Sandrine est **interrompue** par l'arrivée du professeur de mathématiques, qui **remarque** immédiatement la présence de Robin à qui il s'adresse aussitôt: "C'est vous le nouvel élève?" Robin **se lève** et répond: "Oui Monsieur, Je m'appelle Robin Fournier.

Interrompue - ***interrupted***
Remarque (remarquer) - ***notices (to notice)***
Se lève (se lever) - ***stands up (to stand up)***

- Robin! Êtes-vous arrivés aux équations du 3ème degré avec ton ancien professeur?
- Oui!
- Parfait! Tu dois avoir ton **bouquin** avec toi, ouvre-le à la page 45, puis passe au tableau me faire l'exercice numéro 11."

Équations du 3ème degré - ***cubic equations***
Bouquin - ***book***

Le jeune garçon, tout étonné mais **très sûr de lui,** se presse d'aller au tableau et **en moins de temps** qu'il ne faut pour le dire, l'exercice est **résolu.** Le professeur, tout réjoui, dit: "Et bien ça nous change! Enfin! Nous avons quelqu'un de **doué** en maths dans cette classe, qui plus est très poli." Puis il s'adresse à Robin et lui demande: "As-tu une passion particulière pour les maths?

Étonné - ***surprised***
Très sûr de lui - ***very confident***
En moins de temps qu'il ne faut pour le dire - ***in no time***
Résolu (résoudre) - ***solved (to solve)***
Doué - ***gifted***

- Oui Monsieur, c'est l'une de mes **matières** préférées.
- Quelle **note** as-tu eue à ton dernier examen de maths ?

  - J'ai eu un 17/20.
  - Bravo! Tu es sûrement très **studieux** et très **attentif** en classe. Reprends ta place."

Matières - ***subjects***
Note – ***grade/mark***
Studieux - ***studious***
Attentive - ***attentive/paying close attention***

Robin s'exécute et une fois à sa place, sa camarade lui dit qu'il s'est **débrouillé comme un chef.** Elle lui demande s'il est possible qu'elle révise avec lui, car le prof leur impose une **interrogation** surprise par semaine. Robin accepte de réviser avec sa nouvelle amie et lui propose de commencer dès aujourd'hui. Les deux jeunes gens **se mettent d'accord** pour travailler chez Robin après l'école **le jour-même.**

S'est débrouillé comme un chef (se débrouiller comme un chef) - ***managed splendidly (to manage splendidly)***
Réviser - ***to revise/to review***
Interrogation surprise - ***pop quiz***
Se mettent d'accord (se mettre d'accord) - ***agree (to agree)***
Le jour-même - ***the same day***

À la fin de la journée, les deux nouveaux amis, qui ont bien **fait connaissance,** sont ensemble à la maison des Fourniers. **Aussitôt** arrivés, Robin veut se mettre au travail, ce qui n'est pas le cas de Sandrine qui lui dit qu'elle veut **d'abord** visiter la maison, et qu'ils venaient à peine de sortir du lycée. Robin accepte mais lui fait promettre de se mettre au travail juste après la visite, il lui dit qu'il faut être organisé pour avoir de bonnes notes.

Fait connaissance (faire connaissance) - ***gotten acquainted (to get acquainted)***
Aussitôt - ***immediately***
D'abord - ***first***
À peine de - ***hardly***

La visite **terminée**, les parents de Robin **rentrent à la maison** et là, Madame Fournier lui dit: "Je vois que tu t'es vite intégré à ton nouveau lycée. Qui est cette jolie fille?

- Elle s'appelle Sandrine. On est dans la même classe. On va travailler ensemble ce soir.
- Très bien mon fils ! Bonjour Sandrine! Faites comme chez vous."

Terminée - ***finished***
Rentrent à la maison (rentrer à la maison) - ***come home (to come home)***

La jeune fille remercie Madame Fournier et les deux lycéens **se retirent** pour travailler dans la chambre de Robin. Ils sortent leurs **cahiers**, leurs **stylos**et leurs bouquins. Ils passent leur **soirée** avec les maths.

Se retirent (se retirer) - ***withdraw themselves (to withdraw oneself)***
Cahiers - ***notebooks***
Stylos - ***pens***
Soirée - ***evening***

Le lendemain, les deux amis **se revoient** au lycée. Sandrine **remercie** à nouveau Robin pour son aide et pour lui avoir tout **expliqué**. Robin lui dit qu'ils peuvent encore travailler ensemble quand elle le

souhaite.

Se revoient (se revoir) - ***see each other again (to see each other again)***
Remercie (remercier) - ***thanks (to thank)***
Expliqué - ***explained***
Souhaite (souhaiter) – ***hopes/wishes (to hope/to wish)***

En classe, Robin **dévoile l'étendue** de son intelligence et de ses **connaissances**, si bien que certains éléments rebelles commencent à être **jaloux** de lui. Mais bon il ne risque rien, ils sont un peu **zélés** mais pas du tout dangereux.

Dévoile (dévoiler) - ***reveals (to reveal)***
L'étendue - ***the extent***
Connaissances - ***knowledge***
Éléments rebelles - ***rebellious "elements" (euphemism to say "bad students")***
Jaloux - ***jealous***
Zélés - ***zealous***

Le tout dernier cours de l'après-midi s'avère être les mathématiques. Le prof entre et **surprend** toute la classe avec une interrogation surprise. Sandrine, toute **effrayée,** demande à Robin:

Surprend (surprendre) - ***surprises (to surprise)***
Effrayée - ***frightened***

"Tu penses que ça ira avec ce qu'on a étudié hier?

- Oui, le prof a dit que ça portera sur ce qu'on a vu hier en cours, ça tombe bien, c'est ce qu'on a vu chez moi."

Détendue, Sandrine prend **ses affaires** pour **l'interrogation**, le prof donne **les sujets** et l'interrogation commence. Une heure plus tard une autre élève s'occupe de **ramasser** les copies de ses camarades pour le prof.

Ça tombe bien - ***that's a piece of luck***
Affaires - ***stuff***
L'interrogation - ***the quiz***
Les sujets - ***the topics/the themes***
Ramasser - ***to pick up***

"Je vais **corriger** tout ça ce soir et vous aurez vos **notes** demain matin!" dit le prof. Et la seconde journée de Robin dans son nouveau lycée s'achève.

Corriger - ***to correct***
Notes - ***marks/grades***

Le matin de sa troisième journée dans sa nouvelle école, Robin est très attendu en classe, tout le monde est impatient de connaître la note du petit nouveau. "Le prof de maths arrive!" dit un camarade à Robin. Une fois installé, le prof **se met à appeler les** élèves **un par un** pour leur donner leurs copies. "Sandrine Morel! Tu as beaucoup progressé. 13/20." La jeune fille **saute de joie** et court chercher **sa copie.**

Se met à (se mettre à) - ***starts (to start)***
Un par un - ***one by one***
Saute de joie - ***jumps for joy***
Sa copie – ***his/her paper***

En **revenant à sa place,** elle remercie Robin pour son aide. Quelques noms plus tard le prof arrive au dernier nom de la liste qui est celui de Robin étant nouveau: "Robin Fournier! 18,5/20! Vous avez la meilleure note!" Tout le monde est **en admiration** devant Robin, il remarque également que les trois **indisciplinés** de la classe le regardent d'**une drôle de façon**, mais **il n'y prête pas attention**.

Revenant à sa place - ***back in her seat***
En admiration - ***in admiration/in awe***
Indisciplinés - ***Unruly***
Une drôle de façon - ***a very funny way***
Il n'y prête pas attention. - ***he does not pay attention/he ignores it***

Histoire/Story 2: Un nouveau lycée

Le reste de la journée se passe très bien pour Robin. Il se fait beaucoup de nouveaux amis, s'étant fait remarquer, tout le monde vient lui parler. Sandrine n'arrête pas de **faire les éloges de** Robin, et dit à tout le monde que c'est **grâce à** lui qu'elle **a obtenu** cette bonne note. Fabienne, Manon, Jaques, Julien, Samira, Amandine, Jean-Luc, Robin **ne sait plus où donner de la tête.** Il n'arrive pas à retenir tous les noms. La journée se termine par **une sortie** entre amis de la même classe, ils se décident à aller faire du karting en ville. "Cette sortie est l'occasion de **me changer les idées**." se dit Robin.

Le reste - ***the rest***
Faire les éloges de – ***to sing the praises of***
Grâce à - ***thanks to***
A obtenue (obtenir) - ***obtained (to obtain)***
Ne sait plus où donner de la tête - ***does not know which way to turn***
Retenir - ***to remember***
Une sortie - ***an outing***
Me changer les idées - ***to take my mind off things***

Au karting, tout le monde **s'amuse**. Mais Robin, qui n'est pas très **sportif**, ne **s'en sort pas** du tout. "Finalement, tu nes pas doué pour tout. Robin." Lui dit son nouvel ami Julien. Robin lui répond: "Ouais. Je ne suis pas très **manuel**." La soirée se termine bien et Robin rentre chez lui. Au coin d'une **ruelle** il aperçoit trois de ses autres camarades. "Ce sont les trois mauvais éléments de la classe." Se dit Robin. Il **presse le pas** et les évite pour ne pas **faire d'histoires**. Mais après les **avoir dépassés** de quelques mètres, il les entend l'appeler: "Robin ! Robin ! Robin!." Robin se retourne. Les trois **acolytes** s'avancent vers lui, il les attend en **s'attendant au pire**. Et une conversation **démarre** entre lui et ses trois camarades.

S'amuse (s'amuser) – ***is/are having fun (to have fun)***
Sportif - ***athletic***
S'en sort (s'en sortir)- ***manages very well/does well (to manage very well/to do well)***
Manuel - ***practical***
Une ruelle - ***a little street/an alley***
Presse le pas (presser le pas) - ***hurries up/quickens his pace (to***

hurry up/to quicken one's pace)
Faire d'histoires - ***to create drama/rumors***
Avoir dépassés – ***having gone past/having passed***
Acolytes – ***associates/friends***
S'attendant au pire - ***expecting the worst***
Démarre (démarrer) - ***starts (to start)***
Il leur dit: "Oui?!

- Salut Robin, tu ne nous **reconnais** pas?! On est dans la même classe.
- Je vous ai reconnu. Mais je ne savais pas que c'était moi que vous attendiez.
- Si. Bon, d'abord moi , c'est Bastien et voila Kamel et Corentin.
- Enchanté les **mecs** . Vous avez besoin de quelque chose?
- Ouais! Sandrine a dit que tu l'avais aidée à avoir sa bonne note. **On est dans de beaux draps**. On n'arrive pas à **s'en sortir** au lycée, on ne comprend pas les **explications** des profs. Le surveillant nous a déjà **pris** en train de **tricher**. On a déjà été **suspendu** et on risque un **renvoi définitif.** Dis Robin, tu ne veux pas faire comme avec Sandrine et nous aider à avoir de bonnes notes?"

Reconnais (reconnaître) - ***recognize (to recognize)***
Mecs - **guys**
On est dans de beaux draps - ***we are in a right mess***
S'en sortir - ***to manage well/to do well***
Explications - ***explanations***
Pris - ***caught***
Tricher - ***to cheat***
Suspendu - ***suspended***
Renvoi définif - ***expulsion***

Robin, tout étonné, pense qu'il a **tout à gagner** en les aidant, non seulement il ne les aura pas contre lui, et en plus ils **s'amélioreront**. Il réfléchit quelques secondes et leur dit: "Bon ! Je veux bien vous aider. Mais **mettez- vous en tête** qu'il va falloir **vous y mettre** dès demain, et que ça ne sera pas facile.

Histoire/Story 2: Un nouveau lycée

A tout à gagner (avoir tout à gagner) - ***has everything to gain (to have everything to gain)***
S'amélioreront (s'améliorer) - ***will improve themselves (to improve oneself)***
Mettez-vous en tête (se mettre en tête) - ***get it into your heads (to get it into one's head)***
Vous y mettre (se mettre) - ***you start (to start)***

- Merci! Merci infiniment!"

Quelques semaines **se sont écoulées** depuis l'arrivée de Robin dans son nouveau lycée, son arrivée a bénéficié à bon nombre de ses camarades qui ont **changé du tout au tout**. Les examens approchent et **profitant d**'une autorisation du surveillant qui leur accorde une salle après les cours, Robin donne un coup de main à ses camarades en difficulté et tout le monde fait de son mieux.

Se sont écoulées (s'écouler) - ***have passed (to pass)***
À bon nombre de - ***a large number of***
Changé du tout au tout - ***changed completely***
Profitant de - ***taking advantage of***

Le jour des examens est finalement arrivé. Robin, toujours **accolé** à Sandrine, se dirige vers la salle de cours. Tout le monde **s'acharne** à enlever le plus d'informations possible de leurs bouquins. Le professeur arrive et distribue les sujets d'examen. Le premier examen débute. Une semaine plus tard, les résultats sont affichés et **pratiquement** tout le monde a réussi. Robin **est remercié** par toute sa classe, le petit bonhomme est devenu la **coqueluche** du lycée.Lui qui redoutait tellement ce nouveau lycée, a complètement oublié ses **craintes** et il a pu s'y intégrer très rapidement.

Vocabulary Recap 1:

Accolé - ***lumped together/conjoined to***
S'acharne (s'acharner) - ***desperately attempts to (to desperately attempt to)***
Pratiquement - ***almost***
Est remercié (être remercié) - ***is thanked (to be thanked)***
La coqueluche - ***the idol***
Ses craintes - ***his fears/his doubts***

Vocabulary Recap 2:

Déménagée **- (déménager)** - *moved house* ***- (to move house)***
Lycée - ***secondary school/high school***
Rentrée - ***start of the school year***
Proche – ***close/near/nearby***
Enchantait **(enchanter)** - *enchanted* ***- (to enchant)***
Redoutait (redouter) - ***feared (to fear)***
A tardé (tarder) - ***took a long time (to take a long time)***
Traîne (traîner) – ***dawdles/lags behind (to dawdle/to lag behind)***
Voulant à tout prix - ***desperate to***
Cesse (cesser) ***- ceases (to cease)***
Se dépêche (se dépêcher) - ***hurries (to hurry)***
Se préparer - ***to get ready***
Tant bien que mal - ***somehow***
Parvient à - ***manages to***
Indispensable - ***essential***
Rester ***- to stay***
Quartier – ***district/neighborhood***
Rassurant – ***reassuring***
Avale (avaler)- ***swallows (to swallow)***
Se fait remarquer (se faire remarquer) - ***gets noticed (to get noticed)***
S'approche (s'approcher) - ***gets close (to get close)***
L'accueil - ***the welcome/the reception***
Être transféré – ***to be transferred***
Suivez (suivre) - ***follow (to follow)***
Conduire - ***to bring/to take somewhere***
Te plairas (se plaire) — ***will enjoy yourself (to enjoy oneself)***
Au beau milieu de — ***right in the middle of***
Rassure-toi — ***don't worry***

Histoire/Story 2: Un nouveau lycée

Professeur principal - ***homeroom teacher***
Enseignera (enseigner) - ***will teach (to teach)***
Salle de classe - ***classroom***
En chemin - ***on the road/on the way***
Visiter les lieux - ***visit the premises***
Activités extra-scolaires - ***extra-curricular activities***
Frappe (frapper) - ***(to knock)***
En s'adressant au(à) - ***addressing***
Confie (confier) - ***entrust (to entrust)***
Installe-toi (s'installer) - ***sit (to sit)***
Au fond (de la classe) - ***the back (of the class)***
Prendre place - ***to take a seat***
Prononcer - ***to pronounce/to utter/to say***
Le moindre mot (expression) - ***any/a single word (expression)***
Poursuit (poursuivre) - ***carries on with/continues (to carry on with/ to continue)***
Dans le coin - ***in the neighborhood***
Avis - ***opinion***
Méfie - ***distrust***
Tableau - ***board (blackboard)***
Interrompue - ***interrupted***
Remarque (remarquer) - ***notices (to notice)***
Se lève (se lever) - ***stands up (to stand up)***
Équations du 3ème degré - ***cubic equations***
Bouquin - ***book***
Étonné - ***surprised***
Très sûr de lui - ***very confident***
En moins de temps qu'il ne faut pour le dire - ***in no time***
Résolu (résoudre) - ***solved (to solve)***
Doué - ***gifted***
Matières - ***subjects***
Note – ***grade/mark***
Studieux - ***studious***
Attentive - ***attentive/paying close attention***
Réviser - ***to revise/to review***
Interrogation surprise - ***pop quiz***
Se mettent d'accord (se mettre d'accord) - ***agree (to agree)***
Le jour-même - ***the very same day***

Fait connaissance (faire connaissance) - ***gotten acquainted (to get acquainted)***
Aussitôt - ***immediately***
D'abord - ***first***
À peine de - ***hardly***
Terminée - ***finished***
Rentrent à la maison (rentrer à la maison) - ***come home (to come home)***
Se retirent (se retirer) - ***withdraw themselves (to withdraw oneself)***
Cahiers - ***notebooks***
Stylos - ***pens***
Soirée - ***evening***
Se revoient (se revoir) - ***see each other again (to see each other again)***
Remercie (remercier) - ***thanks (to thank)***
Expliqué - ***explained***
Souhaite (souhaiter) – ***hopes/wishes (to hope/to wish)***
Dévoile (dévoiler) - ***reveals (to reveal)***
L'étendue - ***the extent***
Connaissances - ***knowledge***
Éléments rebelles - ***rebellious "elements" (euphemism to say "bad students")***
Jaloux - ***jealous***
Zélés - ***zealous***
Surprend (surprendre) - ***surprises (to surprise)***
Effrayée - ***frightened***
Ça tombe bien - ***that's a piece of luck***
Affaires - ***stuff***
L'interrogation - ***the quiz***
Les sujets - ***the topics/the themes***
Ramasser - ***to pick up***
Corriger - ***to correct***
Notes - ***marks/grades***
Se met à (se mettre à) - ***starts (to start)***
Un par un - ***one by one***
Saute de joie - ***jumps for joy***
Sa copie – ***his/her paper***
Revenant à sa place - ***back in her seat***

Histoire/Story 2: Un nouveau lycée

En admiration - ***in admiration/in awe***
Indisciplinés - ***unruly***
Une drôle de façon - ***a very funny way***
Il n'y prête pas attention. - ***he does not pay attention/he ignores it***
Le reste - ***the rest***
Faire les éloges de - ***to sing the praises of***
Grâce à - ***thanks to***
A obtenue (obtenir) - ***obtained (to obtain)***
Ne sait plus où donner de la tête - ***does not know which way to turn***
Retenir - ***to remember***
Une sortie - ***an outing***
Me changer les idées – ***to take my mind off things***
S'amuse (s'amuser) – ***is/are having fun (to have fun)***
Sportif – ***athletic***
S'en sort (s'en sortir)- ***manages very well/does well (to manage very well/to do well)***
Manuel - ***practical***
Une ruelle - ***a little street/an alley***
Presse le pas (presser le pas) - ***hurries up/quickens his pace (to hurry up/to quicken one's pace)***
Faire d'histoires (faire des histoires) - ***create drama/rumors***
Avoir dépassés – ***having gone past/having passed***
Acolytes – ***associates/friends***
S'attendant au pire - ***expecting the worst***
Démarre (démarrer) - ***starts (to start)***
Reconnais (reconnaître) - ***recognize (to recognize)***
On est dans de beaux draps - ***we are in a right mess***
S'en sortir - ***to manage well/to do well***
Explications - ***explanations***
Pris - ***caught***
Tricher - ***to cheat***
Suspendu - ***suspended***
Renvoi définif - ***expulsion***
A tout à gagner (avoir tout à gagner) - ***has everything to gain (to have everything to gain)***
S'amélioreront (s'améliorer) - ***will improve themselves (to improve oneself)***
Mettez-vous en tête (se mettre en tête) - ***get it into your heads (to***

get it into one's head)
Vous y mettre (se mettre) – ***you start (to start)***
Se sont écoulées (s'écouler) - ***have passed (to pass)***
À bon nombre de - ***a large number of***
Changé du tout au tout - ***changed completely***
Profitant de - ***taking advantage of***
Accolé - ***lumped together/conjoined to***
S'acharne (s'acharner) - ***desperately attempts to (to desperately attempt to)***
Pratiquement - ***almost***
Est remercié (être remercié) - ***is thanked (to be thanked)***
La coqueluche - ***the idol***
Ses craintes - ***his fears/his doubts***

Practice your writing now:

Write a short summary of this story.

Sample:

Après le déménagement de ses parents, Robin n'a pas le choix, il doit changer de lycée. Il **appréhende** beaucoup ce nouveau lycée. Robin **traîne des pieds**, mais il y va quand même.

Appréhende (appréhender) - ***dreads (to dread)***
Traîne des pieds (trainer des pieds) - ***dawdles (to dawdle)***

Arrivé au lycée, une dame de l'administration lui fait visiter l'école avant de le conduire à sa classe où elle le présente à son professeur et ses camarades.

Un petit moment plus tard la voisine de table de Robin, Sandrine, **l'aborde** et discute avec lui. Elle le met en garde contre le prof de mathématiques adepte d'interrogations surprises.

L'aborde (aborder) - ***approaches him (to approach)***

Tout juste arrivé, le prof de maths remarque Robin. Il lui pose des questions sur **l'avancement** des cours. Et il finit en lui demandant de passer au tableau pour résoudre un exercice. Robin **s'en sort** très bien. Son professeur et ses camarades sont tous étonnés. Il s'avère que les maths est l'une des matières préférées de Robin. Sandrine lui demande de l'aider à réviser, car Ils ne sont jamais à l'abri d'une interrogation surprise. Les nouveaux amis révisent ensemble chez Robin le soir même.

Avancement - ***progress***
S'en sort (s'en sortir) - ***manages very well/does well (to manage very well/to do well)***

Le jour suivant, Le prof de maths annonce une interrogation dès son entrée en classe. Les deux amis travaillent bien et à la fin de l'examen le prof leur dit que les résultats seront donnés le lendemain

A la **remise des résultats.** Sandrine obtient une bonne note et Robin obtient la meilleure note. La note de Robin le rend très populaire parmi ses camarades. Le soir même, les nouveaux amis passent la soirée ensemble. À la fin de cette soirée, Robin est même interpelé par des rebelles de sa classe qui lui demandent son aide.

Remise des résultats - ***presentation of results***

Et ainsi, Robin qui redoutait beaucoup son lycée, s'y est parfaitement intégré et aide ses amis en difficulté à préparer leurs examens. Une semaine après les examens, les résultats sont affichés et pratiquement tout le monde a réussi. Robin devient très populaire.

Histoire 3/Story 3: Cuisiner pour le pique-nique

La famille Leclerc organise chaque année sa grande **réunion de famille**. Comme chaque année, la réunion se fait chez les grands-parents. Mais cette année, la réunion ne fait pas **plaisir** à tout le monde. Laura, petite fille des Leclerc, **n'a pas très envie** d´y participer.

Histoire 3/Story 3: Cuisiner pour le pique-nique

Réunion de famille - ***family reunion***
Plaisir - ***pleasure/enjoyment***
N'a pas très envie - ***does not really want***

En effet, cette année, les grands parents organisent un pique-nique. Et qui dit pique-nique, dit chacun cuisine et apporte à manger avec lui. Laura, qui n'aime pas cuisiner, **ne sait pas comment faire** pour **se sauver de cette situation**. Elle ne peut pas **faire appel** à un **traiteur**. Sa **grand-mère** est une trop bonne **cuisinière**, elle va savoir que ce n'est pas **fait maison**.

Ne sait pas comment faire - ***doesn't know what to do***
Se sauver de cette situation - ***to escape this situation***
Faire appel - ***to request***
Traiteur - ***caterer***
Grand-mère– ***grandmother***
Cuisinière - ***cook***
Fait maison - ***home-made***

Même si Laura est trop mauvaise cuisinière, et qu'elle **est habituée à se nourrir uniquement** de **surgelés**, elle ne souhaite pas **rater l'occasion** de revoir toute sa famille. Elle **réfléchit** beaucoup mais ne trouve pas de solution.

Est habitué(e) à (être habitué(e)) - ***is used to (to be used to)***
Se nourrir - ***to feed/to eat***
Uniquement - ***only***
Surgelés - ***frozen food***
Rater l'occasion - ***to miss the opportunity***
Réfléchit (réflechir) - ***is thinking (to think)***

La seule option est d'essayer quelques traiteurs, et de choisir **le meilleur**. **Profitant** de la pause, elle demande à une de ses collègues:

Le meilleur - ***the best***
Profitant - ***taking advantage of***

"Véronique! Dites-moi. Vous ne connaissez pas un traiteur dont la cuisine semble faite maison?

– Non. **De nos jours** les traiteurs travaillent comme à l'**usine.** Ce n'est pas bon **du tout**. Pourquoi cherchez-vous un traiteur?"

De nos jours - ***these days***
Usine - ***factory***
Du tout. - ***at all***

Laura raconte alors son histoire à sa collègue. Véronique **se met à rire** et dit à Laura :

"**Si ce n'est que ça**. Je vais vous aider.

- ☐ M'aider?! Non je ne peux pas accepter. Mais c'est gentil de votre part de proposer de cuisiner pour moi.
- ☐ Cuisiner pour vous?! Je n'ai pas dit ça. Je vais vous apprendre à cuisiner.
- ☐ M'apprendre à cuisiner?! J'ai déjà essayé d'apprendre. Mais je ne **retiens** pas ce qu'on me montre. À chaque fois que j'essaye de reproduire ce que j'ai vu, ça **brûle**.
- ☐ Justement je ne vais pas le faire **moi-même.** C'est vous qui allez cuisiner. Moi, je vais juste vous **apprendre**. Faites-moi confiance.
- ☐ D'accord.
- ☐ C'est pour quand votre réunion de famille?
- ☐ Dimanche prochain.
- ☐ Parfait ! Je viendrai chez vous samedi après-midi. Demain nous allons discuter de la préparation pique-nique. D'accord?
- ☐ Oui. Merci beaucoup Véronique."

Se met à rire (se mettre à rire) - ***starts laughing (to start laughing)***
Si ce n'est que ça - ***if that's all***
M'apprendre - ***to teach me***
Retiens (retenir) - ***remember (to remember)***
Brûle (brûler) - ***burns (to burn)***
Moi-même - ***myself***

Histoire 3/Story 3: Cuisiner pour le pique-nique

En fin de journée, Laura appelle sa mère pour lui demander ce qu'elle doit cuisiner pour le pique-nique: "Allô! Maman?

- Oui. Salut **mon cœur**. Ça va?
- Oui ça va. Papa et toi vous allez bien?
- Nous allons bien, merci ma fille.
- Maman. Dis-moi. Qu'est-ce que je dois préparer pour le pique-nique de samedi?
- Depuis quand tu cuisines toi?
- Depuis aujourd'hui. J'ai une surprise et pas de traiteur! Cette fois, c'est moi qui fais tout.
- D'accord. Et bien **mamie** a dit qu'elle **s'occupait du** dessert et **le reste** est pour nous.
- Ok! Merci Maman. **Embrasse papa de ma part**. À plus."

Mon cœur - ***my dear/my sweety***
Mamie - **grandma**
S'occupait du (s'occuper) - ***would take care of (to take care of)***
Le reste - ***the rest (remaining part)***
Embrasse papa de ma part - ***kiss Dad for me***

À peine a-t-elle **raccroché** avec sa mère que Laura appelle Véronique pour lui apprendre les détails qu'elle vient de recevoir de sa mère. Véronique dit à Laura de **compter sur** elle et qu'elles vont en discuter le lendemain.

À peine - ***as soon as/no sooner***
A Raccroché (raccrocher) – ***hung up (to hang up)***
Compter sur - ***to count on***
Le lendemain Véronique et Laura **se revoient** au travail:
Se revoient (se revoir) - ***see each other again (to see each other again)***
"Bonjour Laura ! Ça va aujourd'hui?

– Ça va merci. Et vous?

- Je vais bien aussi. Je vous ai apporté quelques **recettes** idéales pour un pique-nique. Nous les verrons à la pause.

- Merci Véronique. A tout à l'heure."

Recettes - ***recipes***

Après une bonne matinée de travail, les deux collègues se retrouvent pour déjeuner. Et là, Véronique montre des recettes idéales pour un pique-nique:

"Pour un pique-nique, le plus populaire reste le sandwich. Mais il vous faut innover. Que pensez-vous d'un **cake salé**?

- Oui. Ça m'a l'air parfait. C'est aussi **pratique** pour manger.
- D'accord. Vous le voulez à quoi votre cake?
- J'aime bien le **thon**.
- Ok! Donc un cake au thon. Vous pensez quoi d'une salade en plus du cake?
- Oui. Des petits plats pratiques.
- Vous avez une salade préférée?
- Non pas vraiment. Mon grand-père aime beaucoup le **poisson**.
- D'accord, alors une salade niçoise fera l'affaire.
- Super ! Je vais les **impressionner** avec ça.
- Je vous prépare **une liste de courses** pour tout ça. Vous les ferez samedi matin.
- Merci Véronique."

Cake salé - ***savory cake/loaf***
Ça m'a l'air parfait - ***it looks perfect to me***
Pratique - ***practical***
Le thon. - ***tuna***
Poisson - ***fish***
Impressionner - ***to impress***
Une liste de courses - ***shopping list***

Samedi est vite arrivé. Laura se lève rapidement . Elle se prépare en quelques minutes et elle part faire les courses pour le **repas** du **lendemain**. Véronique arrivera vers 14h30. Ça laisse du temps à Laura pour faire ses courses.

Histoire 3/Story 3: Cuisiner pour le pique-nique

Le repas - ***the meal***
Lendemain - ***the next day***

Laura n'est pas très **habituée** aux **produits frais**. Elle ne connaît que le rayon des surgelés du supermarché. Elle a du mal à trouver les autres rayons. Mais elle arrive **tant bien que mal** à finir ses courses. En rentrant, elle souhaite déjeuner au restaurant. Elle part au restaurant du quartier. Elle y commande le **menu du jour,** qu'elle finit très rapidement. Véronique ne va pas tarder à arriver chez Laura.

Est habitué(e) à (être habitué(e)) - ***is used to (to be used to)***
Produits frais - ***fresh products***
Tant bien que mal - ***somehow***
Menu du jour - ***today's special***

À peine arrivée chez elle, Laura pose ses courses sur la table de la cuisine. Au même moment , quelqu'un sonne à la porte. Elle **se dépêche** d'ouvrir. C'est Véronique:

"Salut Véronique! Entrez.

- Bonjour Laura. Vous avez un bel appartement et une **magnifique** cuisine.
- Oui mais elle ne sert pas beaucoup.
- Je vois ça. Vos **ustensiles** sont encore tout neufs. Vous avez fait les courses.
- Oui. Elles sont sur la table.
- Ok ! On commence tout de suite?
- Non, pas tout de suite. Vous boirez bien quelque chose?
- Oui. Je veux bien un petit café.
- Tout de suite."

Se dépêche (se depêcher) - ***hurries (to hurry)***
Magnifique - ***wonderful/magnificent***
Ustensiles - ***utensils***

Une fois le café terminé, Véronique et Laura vont à la cuisine. Elles mettent des **tabliers**. Puis Véronique **déballe** les **courses**. Tout y est. C'est bon. Elle dit à Laura:

"**Tenez,** lavez les **légumes**." Laura **lave** les légumes pendant que Véronique finit de préparer le reste des aliments.

Tabliers - ***aprons***
Déballe (déballer) - ***unpacks (to unpack)***
Les courses - ***groceries***
Tenez - ***take this***
Lavez (laver) - ***wash (to wash)***
Les légumes - ***the vegetables***

Véronique dit que le cake prend plus de temps à réaliser et qu'il faut donc l'attaquer le premier.

À réaliser : ***to make/to prepare (the cake/loaf)***
Attaquer - ***to start/tackle a task***

"Alors, pour le cake il nous faut de la **farine**, de la **levure**, du thon, des olives, du **gruyère râpé**, du lait, des œufs, un **tout petit peu** d'huile, du poivre et du sel **bien entendu**.

- Quelles quantités?
- 200 grammes de thon, 100 grammes de farine, la même quantité de fromage, 50 grammes d'olives, 3 œufs, un demi-sachet de levure, 10 centilitres d'huile et 10 cl de lait. Prenez tous les ingrédients sauf le thon, les olives et le fromage. Mélangez- les.

  - D'accord. Jusque-là c'est **facile**.
  - Très bien. Allez-y. **Mélangez** bien le tout. Maintenant ajoutez les olives, le gruyère et le thon.
  - Ok !
  - À présent. Il nous faut un moule. Où sont les vôtres ?
  - Là-haut dans le placard.
  - D'accord. **Huilez** un peu **l'intérieur** du **moule**. **Versezy** la **pâte** dans le moule. Mettez dans le **four** à 180°C et **laissez-le cuire** 40 à 45 minutes. Vous voyez que ce n'est pas difficile de cuisiner ?
  - Oui. Quand on est **encadré**. C'est plus simple.

Histoire 3/Story 3: Cuisiner pour le pique-nique

Farine - ***flour***
Levure - ***yeast***
Gruyère rapé - ***grated (Swiss) cheese***
Un tout petit peu - ***a little bit***
Bien entendu - ***of course***
Mélangez (mélanger) - ***mix/stir (to mix/to stir)***
Facile - ***easy***
Huilez (huiler) - ***grease (to lubricate)***
L'intérieur - ***the inside***
Moule - ***baking pan/mold***
Versez (verser) - ***pour (to pour)***
Pâte - ***dough***
Four **-** ***oven***
Laissez-le cuire - ***let it cook***
Encadré - ***supervised/lead***

Pendant que Véronique et Laura préparent les ingrédients pour la salade niçoise, le cake cuit tout **doucement** dans le four.:

Doucement – **gently/slowly**

"Pour une salade, il nous faut du poisson. J'ai vu que vous avez bien fait les courses. Il y a du thon et des **anchois**.

- □ Oui. Nous aimons beaucoup cette salade dans notre famille.
- □ Vous avez bon goût dans votre famille.
- □ Merci.
- □ Pour commencer cette salade, mettez les œufs à bouillir. Et en attendant qu'ils cuisent, vous **découperez** les autres ingrédients.
- □ Ok! Chef.
- □ Comme c'est pour un pique-nique. C'est plus pratique de tout **découper en petits morceaux**. Vous avez déjà lavé les légumes. Apportez-les.

– Les voilà.

- □ Découpez les poivrons, les oignons et les tomates en petits dés. Émiettez le thon et coupez la **laitue** en très **fines lanières.**

- D'accord.
- Maintenant les œufs doivent être cuits. **Enlevez-les** du **feu**, épluchez-les et découpez-les en **rondelles**. Pour les anchois. J'ai vu que vous en avez achetés beaucoup. Coupez-les en deux simplement. Ça fera joli.
- Oui. Cette salade est riche en couleur.
- Prenez un grand saladier. Mettez-y tous les ingrédients avec les olives noires, mais pas encore les œufs. À votre avis il ne **manque** pas quelque chose à notre salade?
- Non. Elle est déjà bien pleine. Je ne vois pas ce qu'il pourrait manquer.
- Mais si, il manque quelque chose ! Il manque la sauce.
- Ah ! Oui ! Je l'ai oubliée.
- Pour faire la sauce de la salade niçoise il nous faut de l'huile d'olives. Je vous en ai apporté.
- Merci Véronique. C'est très gentil de votre part.
- Je vous en prie. Versez un peu d'huile dans un **bol**. Ajoutez-y du **vinaigre**, du sel, du poivreet de la moutarde. **Mélangez-le tout**. Et voilà, votre sauce est prête.
- Ajoutez-là à votre salade. Mélangez encore un peu. Mettez les œufs en rondelles sur le haut. Et voilà c'est prêt."

Anchois - ***anchovy***
Découperez (découper) - ***cut out (to cut out)***
En petits morceaux. - ***into small pieces***
Découperez en petit morceaux (découper en petits morceaux) - ***chop (to chop)***
Émiettez (émietter) - ***crumble (to crumble)***
La laitue - ***lettuce***
Fines - ***thin***
Lanières - ***strips***
Enlevez-les (enlever) - ***remove them (to remove)***
Feu - ***fire***
Épluchez (éplucher) - ***peel (to peel)***
Découpez-les - ***cut them out***
Rondelles - ***slices***

Histoire 3/Story 3: Cuisiner pour le pique-nique

Manque (manquer)- ***is missing (to miss/to be missing)***
Bol - ***bowl***
Vinaigre - ***vinegar***
Mélangez le tout - ***mix it all***

Laura se rend compte qu'il peut être très simple de cuisiner. Véronique rappelle à Laura qu'elle a un cake dans le four. Laura court le **sortir**. Il est enfin prêt:

Sortir - ***to take out/to get out***

"Il sent si bon ! Merci véronique. C'est grâce à vous que j'ai pu faire tout ça.

- Ne me remerciez pas. Maintenant vous n'avez plus besoin de traiteur. Et ne mangez plus de surgelés!"

Véronique ne tarde pas chez Laura. Elle **prend congé** très vite après l'avoir aidéeà **faire la vaisselle**. Après avoir raccompagné Véronique, Laura court prendre son téléphone. Elle appelle sa mère et lui annonce que demain elle apportera plein de bonnes choses à manger. "J'espère que ça sera **mangeable**!

- Mais bien sûr. Je me suis **bien appliquée.**
- D'accord. Je ne demande qu'à goûter moi."

Prend congé (prendre congé) **-** ***takes her leave (to take one's leave)***
Faire la vaisselle - ***to wash the dishes***
Mangeable - ***edible***
Bien appliquée. - ***very diligent***

Le jour du pique-nique est enfin arrivé. Laura part très tôt chez ses grands- parents. Elle y est partie tellement tôt qu'elle est la première arrivée. C'est sa grand-mère qui lui ouvre la porte:

"Bonjour mamie!

- Oh! Bonjour ma petite, tu arrives bien tôt. Entre ma chérie.

- Papi n'est pas là?
- Si. Il est dans le jardin. Il prépare les lieux.
- D'accord, j'irai le voir plus tard. Mamie! Regarde ce que j'ai cuisiné pour le pique-nique.
- Tu as cuisiné? Et non pas ton copain le traiteur?!
- Non c'est bien moi. J'ai pris des cours et voilà.
- Bravo ma petite. Qu'as-tu donc préparé?
- Un cake au thon et une salade niçoise.
- Tout ça?! Bravo tu es un grand chef maintenant. Viens dans la cuisine, fais-moi **goûter** tout ça.
- D'accord."

Aussitôt dans la cuisine, Laura fait goûter ses plats à sa grand-mère, qui les adore. Toute contente, elle court appeler le grand-père de Laura, qui arrive très vite. "Qu'est-ce qui se passe? Ah! Laura tu es déjà arrivée?

- Oui elle est arrivée et elle a cuisiné des **merveilles**. **Goûte**-moi ça."

Goûte (goûter) - ***taste (to taste)***
Merveilles – ***wonders/marvels***

Le grand père goûte et il apprécie énormément. Il dit à sa petite fille: "Tu nous as bien caché ce talent!" Laura lui répond: "Je n'ai pas de talent. J'ai simplement eu un bon prof."

La grand-mère de Laura lui signale que son cake est trop petit. Il ne **suffira** pas à tout le monde. Laura propose d'en faire un autre avant que les autres arrivent.

Suffira (suffire) - ***will be enough/will suffice (to be enough/to suffice)***

Heureusement, la grand-mère de Laura a toujours son **réfrigérateur** et ses **placards** bien remplis. Laura trouve facilement tous les ingrédients. Elle reprend les mêmes étapes toutes seules. Les **gestes** appris la **veille** avec Véronique sont **reproduits**, et en une heure, un deuxième cake sort du four. Les invités étant arrivés ont maintenant une preuve que c'est bien Laura qui a cuisiné ce qu'elle a apporté.

Réfrigérateur - ***refrigerator***
Placards – ***cupboards***
Étapes - ***steps***
Gestes - ***movements/actions***
La veille - ***the day before***
Reproduits - ***reproduced***
Le pique-nique peut enfin commencer.

Vocabulary Recap 3:

Réunion de famille - ***family reunion***
Plaisir - ***pleasure/enjoyment***
N'a pas très envie - ***does not really want***
Ne sait pas comment faire - ***doesn't know what to do***
Se sauver de cette situation - ***to escape this situation***
Faire appel - ***to request***
Traiteur - ***caterer***
Grand-mère – ***grandmother***
Cuisinière - ***cook***
Fait maison - ***home-made***
Est habitué(e) à (être habitué(e)) - ***is used to (to be used to)***
Se nourrir - ***to feed/to eat***
Uniquement - ***only***
Surgelés - ***frozen food***
Rater l'occasion – ***to miss the opportunity***
Réfléchit (réflechir) - ***is thinking (to think)***
Le meilleur - ***the best***
Profitant - ***taking advantage of***
De nos jours - ***these days***
Usine - ***factory***
Du tout. - ***at all***
Se met à rire (se mettre à rire) - ***starts laughing (to start laughing)***
Si ce n'est que ça - ***if that's all***
M'apprendre - ***to teach me***
Retiens (retenir) - ***remember (to remember)***
Brûle (brûler) - ***burns (to burn)***
Moi-même - ***myself***
Mon cœur - ***my dear/my sweety***
S'occupait du (s'occuper) - ***would take care of (to take care of)***
Le reste - ***the rest (remaining part)***
Embrasse papa de ma part - ***kiss Dad for me***
À peine - ***as soon as/no sooner***
A Raccroché (raccrocher) – ***hung up (to hang up)***
Compter sur - ***to count on***
Se revoient (se revoir) - ***see each other again (to see each other again)***

Histoire 3/Story 3: Cuisiner pour le pique-nique

Recettes - ***recipes***
Cake salé - ***savory cake/loaf***
Ça m'a l'air parfait - ***it looks perfect to me***
Pratique - ***practical***
Le thon. - ***tuna***
Poisson - ***fish***
Impressionner - ***to impress***
Une liste de courses - ***shopping list***
Le repas - ***the meal***
Lendemain - ***the next day***
Est habitué(e) à (être habitué(e)) - ***is used to (to be used to)***
Produits frais - ***fresh products***
Tant bien que mal - ***somehow***
Menu du jour - ***today's special***
Se dépêche (se depêcher) - ***hurries (to hurry)***
Magnifique - ***wonderful/magnificent***
Ustensiles - ***utensils***
Tabliers - ***aprons***
Déballe (déballer) - ***unpacks (to unpack)***
Les courses - ***groceries***
Tenez - ***take this***
Lavez (laver) - ***wash (to wash)***
Les légumes - ***the vegetables***
Prêt - ***ready***
Attaquerait (attaquer) - ***started/tackled a task (to start/tackle a task)***
Farine - ***flour***
Levure - ***yeast***
Gruyère rapé - ***grated (Swiss) cheese***
Un tout petit peu - ***a little bit***
Bien entendu - ***of course***
Mélangez (mélanger) - ***mix/stir (to mix/to stir)***
Facile - ***easy***
Huilez (huiler) - ***grease (to lubricate)***
L'intérieur - ***the inside***
Moule - ***baking pan/mold***
Versez (verser) - ***pour (to pour)***
Pâte - ***dough***
Four - ***oven***

Laissez-le Cuire - ***let it cook***
Encadré - ***supervised/lead***
Doucement – **gently/slowly**
Anchois - ***anchovy***
Découperez (découper) - ***cut out (to cut out)***
En petits morceaux. - ***into small pieces***
Découperez en petit morceaux (découper en petits morceaux) - ***chop (to chop)***
Émiettez (émietter) - ***crumble (to crumble)***
La laitue - ***lettuce***
Fines - ***thin***
Lanières - ***strips***
Enlevez-les (enlever) - ***remove them (to remove)***
Feu - ***fire***
Épluchez (éplucher) - ***peel (to peel)***
Découpez-les - ***cut them out***
Rondelles - ***slices***
Manque (manquer)- ***is missing (to miss/to be missing)***
Bol - ***bowl***
Vinaigre - ***vinegar***
Mélangez le tout - ***mix it all***
Sortir - ***to take out/to get out***
Prend congé (prendre congé) - ***takes her leave (to take one's leave)***
Faire la vaisselle - ***to wash the dishes***
Mangeable - ***edible***
Bien appliqué - ***very diligent***
Goûte (goûter) - ***taste (to taste)***
Merveilles – wonders/marvels
Suffira (suffire) - ***will be enough/will suffice (to be enough/to suffice)***
Réfrigérateur - ***refrigerator***
Placards – ***cupboards***
Étapes - ***steps***
Gestes - ***movements/actions***
La veille - ***the day before***
Reproduits - ***reproduced***

Practice your writing:

Write a short summary of this story.

Sample:

Laura est invitée à une réunion de famille chez ses grands- parents. La grand-mère de Laura a prévu un pique-niqueet chacun doit cuisiner. Laura **est dans de beaux draps**. Elle, qui ne sait pas cuisiner, ne trouve pas de solution à son problème.

est dans de beaux draps (être dans de beaux draps) - ***is in a pickle (to be in a pickle)***

Au travail, Laura demande à sa collègue Véronique si elle connaît un bon traiteur. Curieuse, Véronique lui demande pourquoi. Laura lui raconte son histoire. Véronique propose à Laura un coup de main, mais celui-ci sera un cours de cuisine.

Elles se mettent d'accord pour faire un cake au thon et une salade niçoise. Le rendez-vous est fixé pour la veille du jour du pique-nique.

Le jour du rendez-vous est là. Laura part faire les courses. Elle met du temps mais Laura arrive à trouver tout ce qu'il lui faut pour préparer le cake au thon et la salade niçoise.

À peine Laura rentrée chez elle, Véronique arrive. Elles ne tardent pas à se mettre au travail.

Véronique guide Laura d'une façon **digne** des meilleurs professeurs. Elles préparent et mettent à cuire au four le cake au thon, avant de passer à la salade niçoise.

Digne - ***worthy of***

Laura suit les instructions de véronique, découpe les ingrédients... Elle prépare la sauce et fait une magnifique salade. En fin de journée, elle remercie Véronique qui rentre chez elle.

Le jour du pique-nique est enfin arrivé. Laura part très tôt chez ses grands-parents. À peine arrivée, elle fait goûter ses plats à ses grands-parents qui sont fiers de la cuisine de leur petite fille. La grand-mère de Laura lui dit qu'un seul cake ne suffit pas à tout le monde. Laura propose d'en faire un autre **sur le champ**. Et c'est ainsi qu'avec une grande confiance Laura reproduit les mêmes gestes de la veille et cuisine un second cake au thon. Elle a réussit et prouvé ses talents en cuisine. Et le pique-nique peut enfin commencer.

Sur le champ - ***right now***

Histoire 4/Story 4: Un samedi à faire des emplettes

Héloïse et Sophie, amies de **longue date**, passent toutes les deux la soirée ensemble. Les deux **copines s'amusent comme au bon vieux temps**. Le mariage du frère de Sophie **approche à grands pas**. Les jeunes femmes discutent de leurs projets pour ce grand jour:

Histoire 4/Story 4: Un samedi à faire des emplettes

Amies de longue date - ***old friends***
Copines – ***friends***
S'amusent (s'amuser) — ***are having a good time (to have a good time)***
Comme au bon vieux temps - ***like the good old days***
Approche à grands pas (approcher à grands pas)- ***is approaching quickly/is just around the corner (to approach quickly/to be just around the corner)***
"Sophie ! Que vas-tu **porter** à la cérémonie?

- Je ne sais pas encore. Surtout qu'il me faut une autre **tenue** pour la **fête**.
- Deux tenues?! Mais tu peux porter la même robe pour les deux.
- Non! Mon François ne se marie qu'une fois dans sa vie. Il faut **faire** honneur à ça. J'ai pensé à un joli **tailleur** pour la cérémonie à la **mairie** et une petite robe pour après. Tu en penses quoi?
- Oui. C'est une bonne idée. Tu as déjà acheté tes tenues?
- Non. Ça te dit **d**'aller faire les boutiques samedi prochain?
- Ouais. Ça serait sympa. Comme ça je pourrai aussi m'acheter de quoi me mettre pour ce **fameux** mariage."

Porter - ***to wear***
Tenue - ***outfit***
Fête - ***celebration***
Faire honneur à - ***to do justice to***
Tailleur - ***pant suit***
Mairie - ***city hall***
Ça te dit de? - ***You up for?/Do you want to?***
Ça serait sympa - ***it would be nice***
Fameux - ***famous***

Le week-end suivant, comme prévu, Héloïse **frappe** à la porte de Sophie. Elle l'attend depuis un bon moment: "C'est maintenant que tu arrives?" Héloïse répond avec un petit sourire: "Pardon. J'**ai croisé** Myriam et on a discuté un petit peu.

- Tu aurais pu faire plus vite que ça. Allez! On y va.
- Ok **Patron**!"

Frappe (frapper) - ***knocks on (to knock)***
Ai croisé (avoir croisé) - ***bumped into/met/ran into (to bump into/ to meet/to run into)***
Patron - ***boss***

Une fois dehors, Sophie **prévient** Héloïse qu'il faut d'abord aller au supermarché. Comme elle était chez ses parents, Sophie n'avait pas fait de course cette semaine. Elles vont donc au supermarché.

Prévient (prévenir) - ***informs (to inform)***

Sur place, les filles prennent un **caddie**. Elles entrent dans le magasin. Héloïse demande à Sophie si elle a prévu de quoi acheter.Sophie lui dit qu'elle a préparé une liste de courses. Tout d'abord Sophie veut aller au **rayon boulangerie**, car il ne lui reste plus de pain. Au rayon boulangerie le vendeur s'adresse aux filles:

Caddie - ***shopping cart/trolley***
Rayon boulangerie - ***bakery department***
"Bonjour Mesdemoiselles. **Que désirez-vous**?

- Bonjour Monsieur. Donnez-moi deux **baguettes traditions** et un petit pain de campagne.
- Tout de suite Mademoiselle. Tenez, voilà votre pain et votre ticket. Vous payerez à la **caisse** en partant du magasin.
- Merci Monsieur. Au revoir."

Que désirez-vous? - ***What would you like?***
Baguettes traditions - ***traditional baguettes***
Caisse - ***checkout***

Après le pain, Héloïse et Sophie se dirigent vers **le rayon fruits et légumes.** Arrivées au rayon, Héloïse demande:

"Qu'est-ce qu'il te **faut** maintenant?

- 1 kilo de pommes de terre, 500 grammes de tomates, 500 grammes d'oignons, quelques **poivrons** de différentes couleurs, 300 grammes de carottes, 200 grammes de **courgettes**, 1/2 **chou**, une **barquette** de **fraises** et une de **framboises**."

Les fruits et légumes **empaquetés** dans le caddie, Sophie dit à sa copine: "La prochaine étape, c'est le rayon **boucherie** et **boisson**." Les deux jeunes femmes finissent leurs courses et vont à la caisse pour **régler leurs achats.**

Le rayon fruits et légumes - ***the fruit and vegetable department***

Faut - ***need***
Poivrons -***peppers***
Courgettes - ***zucchinis***
Chou - ***cabbage***
Barquette - ***punnet***
Fraises - ***strawberries***
Framboises - ***raspberries***
Empaquetés - ***wrapped***
Rayon de boucherie - ***meat department***
Boisson - ***beverage***
Régler leurs achats - ***to pay for their purchases***

Sophie présente ses courses à la **caissière** pendant qu'Héloïse **se charge** d'aller ranger le caddie à sa place.

"Vous voulez payer par **carte** ou en **espèces**?" demande la caissière. Sophie demande à son tour: "C'est combien pour **le tout**?

- Ça fait 42€ mademoiselle.
- Très bien, en espèces alors. J'ai aussi **un bon de réduction** pour les jus de fruits.
- D'accord. Donnez-moi le tout. Vous voulez **un ticket de caisse**?
- Non merci. **Ce n'est pas la peine.**
- Comme vous voulez. Voici votre **monnaie**, à bientôt.

- Au revoir Madame."

Caissière - ***cashier***
Se charge (se charger) - ***takes care (to take care)***
Carte - ***card***
Espèces - ***cash***
Le tout - ***all***
Un bon de réduction - ***a discount voucher***
Un ticket de caisse - ***a receipt***
Ce n'est pas la peine - ***that is not necessary***
Monnaie - ***change***

Sophie retrouve Héloïse à la sortie du supermarché à qui elle dit: "Je vais aller déposer mes courses chez moi. Tu veux m'attendre ou venir avec moi?" Héloïse répond:

"Je vais te **devancer** à la station. Je vais t'attendre là-bas.

- Ok ! À tout de suite."

Sophie court **déposer** ses courses chez elle alors qu'Héloïse part la première à la station de métro. Une dizaine de minutes plus tard, elles se retrouvent et prennent le métro pour aller en ville.

Devancer - ***to get ahead of***
Déposer - ***to drop off***

Une fois en ville, Sophie décide d'aller acheter le tailleur qu'elle portera à la mairie le jour du mariage de son frère. Héloïse ne tarde pas à remarquer un magasin qui fait un **rabais** de 20% sur ses tailleurs. "**Ce n'est pourtant pas** la période des **soldes**!" dit Sophie. "**Peu importe**! On y va" lui dit sa copine. Le magasin a énormément de choix et à des prix **très abordables.** Sophie est attirée par un beau tailleur beige parfait pour un mariage. Elle **se presse** de demander au vendeur de lui en donner un à sa **taille** pour qu'elle l'essaye. Le tailleur lui **va comme un gant**. Elle décide donc de le prendre sans même en connaître le prix. "Est-il soldé lui aussi?" demande Héloïse, "Oui!" Répond le vendeur. La transaction est rapidement faite. Les filles quittent le premier magasin.

Remarquer - ***to notice***
Un rabais - ***a discount***
Ce n'est pourtant pas ***it's not even***
Soldes - ***sales***
Peu importe - ***whatever***
Très abordables - ***very affordable***
Se presse (se presser) - ***rushes (to rush)***
Taille - ***size***
Va comme un gant - ***fits like a glove (expression meaning, 'It fits perfectly well.')***

À présent, elles partent chercher des robes dans leur magasin habituel. À peine arrivées, elles courent voir la vendeuse. Elles lui demandent de lui montrer les tout derniers modèles arrivés. Robe après robe, Sophie et Héloïse **s'emparent des cabines d'essayage**. Les filles mettent du temps à se décider. Finalement, elles se mettent d'accord sur deux robes rouges presque identiques. Elles seront **les stars** de la fête avec ces robes. Étant des **habituées** du magasin, les filles bénéficient de certains privilèges. Comme les deux robes sont **chères**, les vendeurs laissent les filles acheter les robes à crédit. Néanmoins, les filles préfèrent payer **la moitié du prix à l'achat** et **l'autre moitié** quelques semaines plus tard.

À présent - *now*
À peine arrivéees – ***shortly after having arrived***
S'emparent (s'emparer) - ***seize (to seize)***
Cabines d'essayage - ***dressing rooms/fitting rooms***
Les stars - ***the stars (celebrities)***
Des habituées - ***regular customers***
Chères - ***expensive***
À crédit - ***on credit***
La moitié du prix à l'achat - ***half the price at the point of purchase***
L'autre moitié - ***the other half***

Après l'achat des robes, les filles vont au magasin de **chaussures** pour dépenser plus. Les filles se mettent à essayer paire après paire.

Elles n'arrivent toujours pas à se décider. Au final, aucune des paires de la boutique ne leur **convient**. Elles décident donc d'aller voir dans un autre magasin un peu plus loin. Les choses sont bien différentes dans ce deuxième magasin. Toutes les paires **plaisent** aux filles et elles ont de nouveau du mal à choisir.

Une idée traverse soudain l'esprit d'Héloïse qui ne peut le garder plus longtemps pour elle.

Chaussures - ***shoes***
Conviennent (convenir) - ***suit (to suit)***
Plaisent (plaire) - ***appeal to (to appeal to)***
Une idée traverse l'esprit - ***an idea crosses the mind***

"Sophie. Et si on mettait nos robes? C'est plus simple pour voir quelle paire de chaussures convient.

□ Bonne idée! **Allons-y**."

Allons-y - ***Let's do it***

Les filles trouvent le moyen de mettre les vêtements qu'elles ont achetés plus tôt, et se mettent à essayer les chaussures du magasin. Après une heure d'essayage, les filles choisissent finalement des paires qui leur vont bien. Elles finissent par quitter le magasin avec deux nouvelles paires de chaussures.

Après **deux bonnes heures** passées à débattre de chaussures, Sophie et Héloïse s'accordent une pause déjeuner dans un petit restaurant du centre ville. **À table,** un serveur vient apporter les menus aux deux amies, qui parlent de la suite du programme de leur journée à faire les boutiques : « Qu'est-ce que tu veux acheter de plus Sophie ?

Deux bonnes heures - ***a good two hours***
À débattre (débattre) - ***discussing (to discuss)***
À table - ***on the table***

– Je veux m'offrir quelques bijoux pour mettre en valeur mes nouveaux vêtements. Et toi?

□ Et bien ... Déjà pas de bijoux pour moi. Mais je veux bien que tu m'aides à choisir un cadeau de mariage pour ton frère.
□ Mais non. Tu n'as pas besoin de lui faire de cadeau tu fais partie de la famille.
□ Si. Je ne peux pas me permettre de ne pas faire de cadeau de mariage au frère de ma meilleure amie quand même !
□ D'accord. Fais comme tu veux. Moi je vais lui offrir une **toile** de lui et de sa chérie. Je l'ai faite faire par un artiste à partir d'une de leurs photos.
□ Oh! Quel beau cadeau. **Je suis impatiente** de voir ce que tu m'offriras le jour de mon mariage.
□ Trouve-toi un amoureux, après on verra!
□ **Plus facile à dire qu'à faire**!"

Bijoux - ***jewelry***
Mettre en valeur - ***to highlight/to showcase***
Une toile - ***a canvas***
À partir - ***from***
Je suis impatiente (être impatient) - ***I can't wait/I'm eager (to be eager)***
Plus facile à dire qu'à faire - ***easier said than done***

Les deux amies **sont coupées** par le serveur qui revient chercher leur commande. "Qu'avez-vous choisi?

□ **Avec tout ça, n**ous n'avons même pas lu le menu.
□ Vous voulez que je repasse plus tard?
□ Non. Merci. Apportez-moi **la spécialité du chef,** la même chose pour mon amie et une bouteille de vin pour accompagner le tout s'il-vous-plaît.
□ C'est noté!"

Sont coupées (être coupé) – ***are interrupted (to be interrupted)***
Avec tout ça - ***with all of this***
La spécialité du chef - ***Chef's specialty***

Et le serveur repart. Un petit moment plus tard, il revient avec la commande de Sophie et d'Héloïse. Les filles dégustent leur repas en passant un bon moment. Une fois le repas terminé, Sophie, voulant faire plaisir à sa copine, **paye la note** du restaurant. Et elles repartent chercher d'autres **bonnes affaires**.

Paye la note (payer la note) - ***pays the bill (to pay the bill)***
Bonnes affaires - ***good deals***

En route, Héloïse demande à Sophie s´il y a une **bijouterie** où elle veut faire ses achats. Sophie répond que non et lui demande si elle en connaît une bonne. C'est alors qu'Héloïse lui parle de la bijouterie de son oncle, qui se trouve à quelques **centaines** de mètres de là où elles sont. Sophie dit à son amie: "Mais oui! Ton oncle est **bijoutier**. Il a de belles choses?

Bijouterie - ***jewelry store/jewellery shop***
Centaines - ***hundreds***
Bijoutier - ***jeweler (jeweller)***

- Je ne peux pas te répondre. Ça fait bien longtemps que je ne suis plus allée dans son magasin. Mais vu tous les bijoux que porte ma tante. ,Je pense pouvoir te dire qu'il a de jolies choses.
- Allons voir ça. Ça ne nous coûte rien d'aller voir.
- D'accord. Suis-moi, c'est par là."

Sophie suit son amie qui la mène à la boutique de son oncle, qui est bien content de revoir sa nièce: "En voilà une surprise! Ça doit faire plus de cinq ans que tu n'as pas **montré le bout de ton nez** ici.

- Salut **Tonton**. Comment vas-tu?
- Moi, je vais bien merci. Et toi, **qu´est-ce qui t'amène par ici**?
- Je te présente mon amie Sophie. Tu dois **te souvenir** d'elle. Elle souhaite s'offrir quelques bijoux pour le mariage de son frère.

– Mais oui, bien sûr, la petite Sophie. **Tu as beaucoup grandi**.. Attendez-moi un instant les filles, je vais vous chercher mes meilleures pièces."

Montré le bout de ton nez (montrer le bout du nez) - ***showed up (to show up)***
Tonton - ***Uncle***
Qu´est-ce qui t'amène par ici? - ***what brings you here?***
Te souvenir - ***remember***
Tu as beaucoup grandi - ***you've grown a lot***

Et le vieil homme se retire pour chercher ses merveilles. "Il est toujours aussi gentil ton oncle. Et sa boutique est très belle » dit Sophie à Héloïse. Le vieux bijoutier revient **les bras chargés** de boîtes qu'il pose sur le **comptoir** avant de les ouvrir. Sophie est immédiatement attirée par un petit **collier** en or avec un charmant **pendentif serti** de **pierres** blanches. Elle demande au bijoutier si elle peut l'essayer. Le bijoutier accepte et le lui met. Elle court se regarder dans un miroir et elle le trouve magnifique sur elle. Elle lui demande:

Merveilles – ***wonders/marvels***
Les bras chargés - ***arms full***
Comptoir - ***counter***
Collier - ***necklace***
Pendentif - ***pendant***
Serti – ***set***
Pierres - ***stones***
"Combien coûte-t-il?

- Il est gratuit!
- Comment?!
- Et bien il coûte 0€. Je vous l'offre.
- Mais je ne peux pas accepter. C'est sûrement trop cher.
- J'insiste. Prenez-le comme un cadeau pour le mariage de votre frère. Il faut bien fêter la visite de ma nièce et de la petite Sophie.
- Merci Monsieur. Merci infiniment."

Heureuse, Sophie quitte le magasin,toujours accompagnée de sa meilleure amie, qu'elle **ne cesse** de remercier. Héloïse la **somme** d'arrêter ses remerciements et de se concentrer sur une idée pour le cadeau de mariage. Sophie lui dit: "Prends-lui une chemise. Il sera content.

Ne cesse de (ne pas cesser de) - **keeps on (to keep on)**
Somme (sommer) – **orders/tells (to order/to tell)**

- Non je veux quelque chose qu'il puisse utiliser avec sa femme, comme **une parure de lit**. Tu en penses quoi?
- C'est une bonne idée. Il y a une **grande surface** pas très loin d'ici. On y va?

– D'accord."

Une parure de lit - ***a set of bed linen***
Grande surface - ***supermarket***

Les deux amies vont à la grande surface. Et ne tardent pas à trouver la **section réservée au linge de maison.** "Je ne veux pas quelque chose de trop simple."avoue Héloïse. "Tu penses quoi de la marron là-bas? C'est la couleur préférée de François. »

Section réservée au - ***section reserved for***
Linge de maison - ***household linen***

- Elle est jolie. Allons la voir de plus près. Ouais elle est pas mal et il a tout ce qu'il faut. Tu penses que les mariés aimeront?
- J'en suis certaine. Prends-la.
- Ok! Allons la payer et la faire **emballer**."

Emballer - ***to pack***

Le cadeau emballé et payé, les filles quittent le magasin. La journée de shopping se termine pour les deux amies, qui repartent à la station de métro pour rentrer chez elles, les bras chargés de paquets.

Vocabulary Recap 4:

Amies de longue date - ***old friends***
Copines – ***friends***
S'amusent (s'amuser) — ***are having a good time (to have a good time)***
Comme au bon vieux temps - ***like the good old days***
Approche à grands pas (approcher à grands pas)- ***is approaching quickly/is just around the corner (to approach quickly/to be just around the corner)***
Porter - ***to wear***
Tenue - ***outfit***
Fête - ***celebration***
Faire honneur à - ***to do justice to***
Tailleur - ***pant suit***
Mairie - ***city hall***
Ça te dit de? - ***You up for?/Do you want to?***
Ça serait sympa - ***It would be nice***
Fameux - ***famous***
Frappe (frapper) - ***knocks on (to knock)***
Ai Croisé (avoir croisé) - ***bumped into/met/ran into (to bump into/ to meet/to run into)***
Patron - ***boss***
Prévient (prévenir) - ***informs (to inform)***
Caddie - ***shopping cart/trolley***
Rayon boulangerie - ***bakery department***
Que désirez-vous? - ***What would you like?***
Baguettes traditions - ***traditional baguettes***
Caisse - ***checkout***
Le rayon fruits et légumes - ***the fruit and vegetable department***
Faut - ***need***
Poivrons -***peppers***
Courgettes - ***zucchinis***
Chou - ***cabbage***
Barquette - ***punnet***
Fraises - ***strawberries***

Framboises - ***raspberries***
Empaquetés - ***wrapped***
Rayon de boucherie - ***meat department***
Boisson - ***beverage***
Régler leurs achats - ***to pay for their purchases***
Caissière - ***cashier***
Se charge (se charger) - ***takes care (to take care)***
Carte - ***card***
Espèces - ***cash***
Le tout - ***all***
Un bon de réduction - ***a discount voucher***
Un ticket de caisse - ***a receipt***
Ce n'est pas la peine - ***that is not necessary***
Monnaie - ***change***
Devancer - ***to get ahead of***
Déposer - ***to drop off***
Remarquer - ***to notice***
Un rabais - ***a discount***
Ce n'est pourtant pas ***it's not even***
Soldes - ***sales***
Peu importe - ***whatever***
Très abordables - ***very affordable***
Se presse (se presser) - ***rushes (to rush)***
Taille - ***size***
Va comme un gant - ***fits like a glove (expression meaning, 'It fits perfectly well.')***
À présent - ***now***
À peine arrivéees – ***shortly after having arrived***
S'emparent (s'emparer) - ***seize (to seize)***
Cabines d'essayage - ***dressing rooms/fitting rooms***
Les stars - ***the stars (celebrities)***
Des habituées - ***regular customers***
Chères - ***expensive***
À crédit - ***on credit***
La moitié du prix à l'achat - ***half the price at the point of purchase***
L'autre moitié - ***the other half***

Histoire 4/Story 4: Un samedi à faire des emplettes

Chaussures - ***shoes***
Conviennent (convenir) - ***suit (to suit)***
Plaisent (plaire) - ***appeal to (to appeal to)***
Une idée traverse l'esprit - ***an idea crosses the mind***
Allons-y - ***Let's do it***
Deux bonnes heures - ***a good two hours***
À débattre (débattre) - ***discussing (to discuss)***
À table - ***on the table***
Bijoux - ***jewelry***
Mettre en valeur - ***to highlight/to showcase***
Une toile - ***a canvas***
À partir - ***from***
Je suis impatiente (être impatient) - ***I can't wait/I'm eager (to be eager)***
Plus facile à dire qu'à faire - ***easier said than done***
Sont coupées (être coupé) – ***are interrupted (to be interrupted)***
Avec tout ça - ***with all of this***
La spécialité du chef - ***Chef's specialty***
Paye la note (payer la note) - ***pays the bill (to pay the bill)***
Bonnes affaires - ***good deals***
Bijouterie - ***jewelry store/jewellery shop***
Centaines - ***hundreds***
Bijoutier - ***jeweler (jeweller)***
Montré le bout de ton nez (montrer le bout du nez) - ***showed up (to show up)***
Tonton - ***Uncle***
Qu´est-ce qui t'amène par ici? - ***what brings you here?***
Te souvenir - ***remember***
Tu as beaucoup grandi - ***you've grown a lot***
Merveilles – ***wonders/marvels***
Les bras chargés - ***arms full***
Comptoir - ***counter***
Collier - ***necklace***
Pendentif - ***pendant***
Serti – ***set***
Pierres - ***stones***

Ne cesse de (ne pas cesser de) - **keeps on (to keep on)**
Somme (sommer) – **orders/tells (to order/to tell)**
Une parure de lit - ***a set of bed linen***
Grande surface - ***supermarket***
Section réservée au - ***section reserved for***
Linge de maison - ***household linen***
Emballer - ***to pack***

Practice your writing now:

Write a short summary of this story. Do not paraphrase.

Sample:

Lors d'une soirée, Sophie et Héloïse discutent de quoi mettre pour le mariage du frère de Sophie. Sophie dit à son amie qu'elle doit s'acheter deux tenues et qu'elles doivent aller faire les magasins.

Le weekend suivant, les deux amies se revoient. Avant d'aller faire les magasins, Sophie veut passer au supermarché pour y faire quelques courses. Une liste à la main, les filles finissent leurs courses assez vite et repartent.

Sophie et Héloïse prennent le métro pour aller en ville. Une fois arrivées, les deux amies ne tardent pas à trouver de bonnes affaires : tailleur avec 20 % de réduction, robes achetées à crédits et belles chaussures assorties. Les filles dévalisent les boutiques et dépensent beaucoup.

Elles s'accordent une pause pour le déjeuner avant de reprendre leur shopping.

Après le repas, Héloïse conduit Sophie, qui voulait un bijou chez son oncle bijoutier. Arrivées chez le vieux bijoutier, les filles sont très bien accueillies.

L'oncle d'Héloïse **se plie en quatre** pour ces deux visiteuses au point d'offrir un beau collier en or à Sophie qui refuse au début, mais qui finit par l'accepter.

Se plie en quatre - ***bends over backwards***

La journée se poursuit par l'achat d'un cadeau de mariage de la part d'Héloïse. Après quelques hésitations, elle choisit d' acheter une parure de lit.

Sophie propose d'aller dans une grande surface pour en acheter une. Héloïse choisit son cadeau, elle le fait emballer, le paye et les filles repartent. La journée shopping s'achève pour les filles qui repartent chacune avec pleins de paquets.

Histoire 5/Story 5: L'amour sauveur

"Je serai toujours à tes **côtés**!" "Je t'aimerai pour toujours!" "Tu es l'amour de ma vie!" Ces phrases **reviennent à l'esprit** d'Arnaud, elles lui ont toutes été dites par son ancienne petite amie.

À tes côtés - ***by your side***
Reviennent à l'esprit (revenir à l'esprit) - ***come to mind (to come to mind)***

Voilà maintenant cinq ans que son amour **a perdu la vie** dans un terrible **accident de la route**. Même après cinq ans de séparation, Arnaud n'a jamais cessé de l'aimer. **Négligeant** sa vie sociale, Arnaud vit dans le souvenir des **belles années** qu'il a passées avec l'amour de sa vie.

A perdu la vie (perdre la vie) - ***lost her life (to lose one's life/to die)***
Accident de la route - ***road accident***
Négligeant - ***neglecting***
Belles années - ***good times***

Hormis sa famille et son ami **intime** Olivier, Arnaud ne voit plus personne. Sa vie est un **cercle réduit** entre son travail et chez lui. Olivier ne ménage pas ses efforts pour sortir son ami de ce **malheureux état**: **rendez-vous arrangés**, thérapies, **sorties forcées** ... **Mais rien n'y fait**. Le sourire d'Arnaud semble être disparu pour toujours.

Hormis - ***except for/apart from***
Intime - ***close friend***
Cercle réduit - ***reduced/restricted circle***
Malheureux état - ***miserable state***
Rendez-vous arrangés - ***arranged meetings***
Sorties forcés - ***forced hangouts***
Mais rien n'y fait - ***but it's no use***

Un autre samedi soir, Olivier va chez Arnaud pour essayer de le faire **sortir de sa bulle.** Arrivé chez Arnaud, Olivier y trouve Lisa, la petite sœur d'Arnaud. Elle aussi se donne beaucoup de mal pour aider son frère. Assis sans rien faire comme à son habitude, Arnaud **ne prête pas** beaucoup attention à ses visiteurs. Lisa s'occupe d'accueillir Olivier :

Sortir de sa bulle - ***to become widespread***
Ne prête pas (ne pas prêter attention) - ***does not pay attention (to not pay attention)***
"Bonsoir Olivier. Comment vas-tu?

- Ça va merci. Et toi, ça va?
- Oui, ça va. La semaine était un peu longue mais bon j'y suis habituée.
- Comment va-t-il?
- **Toujours au même point**."

Olivier se dirige vers son ami en lui disant: "Coucou Arnaud! Alors? **La forme?**

Toujours au même point. - ***haven't changed***
La forme? - ***Are you okay?***

- Salut Olivier! Ç**a peut aller**. Et toi?
- Ça va super. Alors, prêt à passer une bonne soirée?
- Encore un plan pour me traîner dehors de force?
- Tout à fait **mon cher**. Tues prêt?
- Je suppose que je n'ai pas le choix. **Sinon** Lisa et toi vous allez me **harceler** toute la soirée.

– Ah! Tu vois? Tu peux être malin quand tu veux bien. Lisa, tu te prépares, on y va?"

Ça peut aller - ***it's okay***
Mon cher - ***my dear***
Sinon - ***otherwise***
Harceler - ***to harass***

Tout de suite après, tout le monde prend sa **veste**et se retrouve dehors. Là, Arnaud demande à Olivier:

"Où est-ce qu'on va? J'espère que tu ne vas pas m'emmener dans un endroit trop **bruyant**.

- Non, je t'emmène dans un endroit très spécial.
- Ah bon! Où ça?!
- C'est une surprise!"

En effet, pour aider **efficacement** son meilleur ami, Olivier a prévu quelque chose de radical, quelque chose à laquelle personne **ne s'attend**. Après un petit **trajet** en voiture, Olivier s'arrête et demande à tout le monde de descendre. "Nous y voilà!" Annonce Olivier. "Où sommes-nous?!" demande Arnaud. "Regarde en face!" Lui répond Olivier. "**Orphelinat** st. Joseph! Qu'est-ce qu'on va faire ici?

Histoire 5/Story 5: L'amour sauveur

Veste - ***jacket***
Bruyant - ***noisy***
Efficacement - ***efficiently***
Ne s'attend - ***no one is expecting***
Trajet - ***ride***
Orphelinat - ***orphanage***

- Lisa, tu peux aller chercher les sacs qu'il y a dans le **coffre**?
- Oui!
- Nous sommes ici ce soir pour du **bénévolat**. Une nouvelle amie à moi m'en a parlé, elle travaille ici. Je me suis dit que ça serait mieux de passer la soirée à aider les autres plutôt que d'aller **s'amuser** entre nous.
- Olivier ! Qu'as- tu **derrière la tête**? Je te connais depuis toujours et faire de bonnes actions ne te ressemble pas.
- Ah! Tu me **vexes** en disant ça! C'est juste que mon amie, Louise, avait besoin d'**un coup de main**. En plus ça me permet de te sortir de ton appartement. J'ai apporté quelques **jouets,** ça fera plaisir aux enfants. Allons-y."

Coffre - ***trunk***
Bénévolat - ***charity work/volunteering***
S'amuser - ***to have fun***
Derrière la tête - ***in mind***
Vexes (vexer) – ***offend/hurt (to hurt)***
Un coup de main - ***some help***
Jouets - ***toys***

Arnaud, n'ayant pas trop le choix, **s'exécute**. Une fois à l'intérieur de l'orphelinat, les enfants courent **accueillir** les visiteurs venus les voir. Lisa s'abaisse pour leur parler: "Bonsoir les enfants! On a plein de jouets et de **friandises** pour vous. On espère que vous aimez bien ça." Les enfants aux anges font un **vacarme** énorme.

S'exécute (s'exécuter) - ***complies (to comply)***
Accueillir - ***to welcome***
Friandises – ***candies/sweets***
Vacarme - ***racket***

A ce moment, Louise, l'amie d'Olivier, court voir ce qui se passe:

- "Qu'est-ce qu'il y a les enfants? Pourquoi vous faites autant de bruit?"

Les trois visiteurs **lèvent** la tête pour **apercevoir** une magnifique jeune femme. Elle avait de longs cheveux **raides** d'un **brun profond**, de grands yeux **noisettes** clairs et **lumineux**, elle était mince et grande comme il le fallait. Elle avait un style vestimentaire simple et portait un beau **tablier** rose.

Lèvent (lever) - ***raise (to raise)***
Apercevoir - ***to notice***
Raides - ***straight***
Brun profound - ***deep brown***
Noisettes (adjective) – ***hazel***
Lumineux - ***bright***
Tablier - ***apron***

En voyant qui étaient venus, Louise **affiche** un grand sourire, ce qui en **ajoute beaucoup à son charme**. Elle avance vers ses visiteurs et leur dit:

Affiche un grand sourire (afficher un grand sourire) – ***displays/shows a big smile (to show a big smile)***
Ce qui en ajoute beaucoup à son charme - ***adds a lot to her charm***

"Bonsoir tout le monde. Comment allez-vous? Ce sont tes amis, Olivier?

- Salut Louise. Oui, ce sont mes amis. Voilà Arnaud et elle, c'est sa petite sœur Lisa.
- Enchantée les amis. Bienvenue à St. Joseph."

La jeune femme **se met à faire visiter** les lieux aux trois visiteurs. Là, Arnaud interpelle Olivier **en** lui **chuchotant**: "Je comprends maintenant d'où te vient cette **soudaine** envie de faire de bonnes actions! Ton but c'est de charmer la belle Louise!

Se met à faire visiter (se mettre à) - ***begins giving them a tour of (to start/to begin)***
En chuchotant - ***by whispering***
Soudaine - ***sudden***

- Mon pauvre Arnaud! Ton raisonnement est complètement faux. Il y a bien une raison pour laquelle nous sommes venus ce soir. Mais je te la dirai plus tard."

La soirée se passe bien dans cet orphelinat, les enfants, qui sont très énergiques, ne **manquent** pas d'imagination pour jouer avec leurs visiteurs. Même Arnaud **s'implique du mieux qu'il le peut**.

La fin de la soirée arrive, les trois amis doivent partir et les enfants doivent aller au lit. Les enfants ne veulent pas laisser leurs **bienfaiteurs** partir.

Manquent (manquer) **miss (to miss)**
S'implique - ***involves himself***
Du mieux qu'il le peut. - ***as best he can***
Bienfaiteurs - ***benefactors***

Et au moment de quitter l'orphelinat, un petit garçon pleurant, court vers Arnaud et le **serre** contre lui en disant: "Tu ne veux pas rester avec nous?" Arnaud **s'agenouille** pour **se mettre à la taille du** petit garçon et lui dit **en** lui **souriant**: "Ne t'inquiète pas mon petit. Nous reviendrons te voir."

Serre (serrer) - ***holds (to hold)***
S'agenouille (s'agenouiller) - ***kneels down (to kneel down)***
Se mettre à la taille du - ***to get to the height of***
En souriant - ***while smiling***

Lisa et Olivier **s'étonnent**, Arnaud a **souri**! Lui qui ne l'avait pas fait depuis cinq ans. Toute émue, Lisa court vers son frère et s'agenouille à son tour. Elle serre son grand frère et le petit garçon dans ses bras en disant: "Oui nous reviendrons bientôt. Et même très souvent." Quelques minutes après, les amis s'en vont.

S'étonnent (s'étonner) - ***are surprised (to be surprised)***
A souri (sourire) - ***smiled (to smile)***

En voiture, Arnaud **affiche une mine** plus sereine **que d'habitude**. Et il demande soudainement à Olivier: "Maintenant qu'on est parti de l'orphelinat, tu peux me dire quelle est la raison qui t'a poussée à **faire le bien tout à coup**?

Affiche une mine (afficher une mine) - ***shows a look (to show a look)***
Sereine – ***relaxed/chilled***
Que d'habitude - ***than usual***
Faire le bien - ***to do good deeds***
Tout à coup - ***all of a sudden***

- C'est Louise et toi en même temps!
- Hein?! Comment ça?
- Et bien Louise **n'en a pas l'air comme ça** mais elle est **veuve**. Elle a perdu son mari et sa fille dans un accident de voiture, il y a trois ans! Tout comme toi elle a beaucoup souffert. Mais elle, elle **s'en est remise**.
- Attends, tu essayes de me manipuler pour ça?! Je n'irai plus jamais dans cet endroit. Et je ne veux rien savoir de cette femme!
- Si on y retournera. N'oublie pas ta promesse au petit garçon. De plus je ne te laisse pas le choix."

N'en a pas l'air comme ça (avoir l'air) - ***may not look like it (to look/ to seem)***
Veuve - ***widow***
S'en est remise (se remettre) - ***got over it (to get over)***

Olivier, étant **plus âgé** qu'Arnaud, a toujours **fait figure de** grand frère pour lui. Arnaud lui voue une grande admiration et beaucoup de respect. C'est pour ça qu'il lui **obéit presque au doigt et à l'œil.**

Plus âgé - ***older***
Fait figure de - ***is seen as/is thought of as (to be seen as/to be thought of as)***

Obéit presque au doigt et à l'œil (obéir) – ***obeys his almost every order (to obey)***

Le week-end se termine normalement pour Arnaud. Et une nouvelle semaine débute pour lui. Il passe beaucoup de temps à penser à l'expérience de l'orphelinat et à ce que lui a dit Olivier sur Louise. Arnaud a du mal à s'imaginer comment peut-on vivre normalement après **la perte** de sa famille.

La perte - ***the loss***

Les jours passent et Arnaud ne cesse de penser à Louise et à l'orphelinat. Il arrive pour une fois à penser à autre chose qu'à ses **peines**. Après beaucoup de réflexions, Arnaud décide d'aller voir Louise. Il prend la décision d'aller voir une femme qu'il **vient tout juste de** connaître pour lui parler de ce qu'il ressent.

Peines - ***sorrows***
Vient tout juste de (venir tout juste de) - ***has just (to have just)***

Durant la pause de midi, Arnaud prend un bus qui le mène à l'orphelinat St. Joseph. Une fois sur place, Arnaud **met du temps** avant de frapper à la porte. C'est Louise qui lui ouvre la porte, toujours avec le même sourire **radieux**: "Bonjour! Entrez vite. Il fait froid dehors." A l'intérieur, Arnaud **remarque** qu'il n y a aucun enfant et demande:

Met du temps (mettre du temps) - ***takes time (to take time)***
Radieux - ***radiant***
Remarque (remarquer) - ***notices (to notice)***

"Les enfants ne sont pas là?

- Non les plus grands sont à l'école et les plus petits font leur sieste.
- D'accord. Excusez-moi de venir les mains vides. Dans la hâte, je n'ai pas pensé à apporter quelque chose pour les petits.
- Ce n'est pas grave les visites font beaucoup plaisir aux en-

fants. Ils vous ont déjà adoptés. Ils me demandent tout le temps. Quand est-ce que vous allez revenir les voir?

- Très bien alors. Nous viendrons les voir souvent. En fait Louise, 'est vous que je suis venu voir aujourd'hui.
- Ah bon?! Que puis-je faire pour vous?
- J'espère que ça ne vous **fâchera** pas. Mais grâce à Olivier, je connais votre histoire et celle de la perte de votre famille.
- Non. Ça ne me vexe pas du tout. Je connais votre histoire à vous aussi. Je suis vraiment désolée. C'est terrible de perdre quelqu'un qu'on aime. Je sais ce que c'est.
- Justement Louise. Comment faites-vous pour survivre? **Je n'y arrive pas.** Aidez-moi s'il vous plaît.
- Ce n'est pas simple mais le temps fait bien les choses. En plus, avec mon travail, je n'ai pas le droit de **cesser de vivre**. Ces enfants , eux non plus , n'ont plus leurs familles. Je n'ai pas le droit de les **abandonner**.
- Je vois!
- **Vous voulez vous en sortir**? Venez ici aussi souvent. Je vous guiderai. Faites-moi confiance!"

Fâchera (fâcher) - ***will anger (to anger)***
Je n'y arrive pas - ***I can't do it***
Cesser de vivre - ***to stop living***
Abandonner - ***to abandon/to give up on***
Vous voulez-vous en sortir? - ***Do you want to manage this situation well?***

Les mois **suivants,** il y a eu de nombreuses visites à l'orphelinat de la part d'Arnaud, d'Olivier et parfois de Lisa. À chaque fois, les enfants les attendent avec impatience devant la porte. Peu à peu la magie de **l'enfance** fait **reprendre goût à la vie** à Arnaud, qui **renoue des liens** avec le rire et la joie. Il **se familiarise** avec le bonheur que lui donnent ces petits enfants.

Suivants – ***following***
Enfance - ***childhood***
Reprendre goût à la vie - ***to rediscover a taste for life***
Renoue des liens (renouer les liens) - ***renews the ties (to renew the ties)***

Se familiarise - ***familiarizes (to familiarize with)***

Par la même occasion, Arnaud **renoue avec des sentiments oubliés.** Eh oui ! La belle Louise ne le laisse pas indifférent. Se disant qu'il ne peut plus **se laisser aller** et qu'il doit se relever, il fait de son mieux pour **nouer** des liens forts avec elle. Il l'invite même à sortir avec lui : une première fois au restaurant, la seconde fois au cinéma et ainsi de suite. Les mois passent et les deux amoureux ne se quittent plus.

Renoue avec des sentiments oubliés (renouer avec des sentiments oubliés) - ***reconnects with forgotten feelings (to catch up/reconnect with forgotten feelings)***
Se laisser aller - ***to go with the flow***
Nouer des liens forts - ***to develop close ties/to build strong ties***
Sortir - ***to go out***

Arnaud, sachant que la vie est trop courte, décide de **demander Louise en mariage**. Il en parle à sa famille et ses amis. Ils **accueillent la nouvelle avec joie**. Il décide donc d'inviter Louise à sortir pour lui faire sa demande. Il prévoit un **cadre** très romantique avec un dîner **en plein air** et un violoniste.

Demander en mariage - ***to propose***
Accueillent la nouvelle avec joie (accueillir la nouvelle) - ***greet the news with joy (to greet the news)***
Un cadre - ***a setting***
En plein air - ***outdoors***

Vers la fin du dîner, Arnaud invite Louise à danser. Elle accepte. Durant cette danse, Arnaud lui parle et lui dit: "Tu as le pouvoir de me faire **revenir à la vie**. Aujourd'hui, grâce à toi, je crois en la vie. Je crois en notre amour. Je t'aime tellement ma Louise. Je ne veux pas me séparer de toi. Je ne veux pas vivre loin de toi. **C'est pour cela que**..."

Revenir à la vie - ***to come back to life***
C'est pour cela que - ***that is why***

À ce moment précis le violoniste change de musique. Il joue **l'air préféré** de Louise, pendant qu'Arnaud s'agenouille et sort une petite boîte ronde rouge. Il regarde Louise et lui dit: "Louise! Ma belle Louise. Tu es mon **ange sauveur** et pour ça je ne peux plus vivre loin de toi. Veux-tu m'épouser?" Louise, **en larmes** et toujours avec le même sourire **radieux** lui répond "Oui! Oui! Oui!"

L'air préféré - ***the favorite tune***
Ange sauveur - ***guardian angel***
En larmes - ***in tears***
Radieux - ***bright/radiant***

Olivier, qui n'a jamais abandonné son copain, a réussi le **pari fou** de le **libérer de l'emprise du passé**. Et depuis Arnaud et Louise **courent des jours heureux** dans l'orphelinat St. Joseph entourés de leurs nombreux enfants.

Pari fou - ***crazy bet***
Libérer de l'emprise du passé. - ***to free from the grip of the past***
Courent des jours heureux (courir des jours heureux) - ***are enjoying happy days (to enjoy happy days)***

Vocabulary Recap 5:

À tes Côtés - ***by your side***
Reviennent à l'esprit (revenir à l'esprit) - ***come to mind (to come to mind)***
A perdu la vie (perdre la vie) - ***lost her life (to lose one's life)***
Accident de la route - ***road accident***
Négligeant - ***neglecting***
Belles années - ***good times***
Hormis - ***except for/apart from***
Intime - ***close friend***
Cercle réduit - ***reduced/restricted circle***
Malheureux état - ***miserable state***
Rendez-vous arrangés - ***arranged meetings***
Sorties forcées - ***forced hangouts***
Mais rien n'y fait - ***but it's no use***
Sortir de sa bulle - ***to become widespread***
Ne prête pas attention (ne pas prêter attention) - ***does not pay attention (to not pay attention)***
Toujours au même point. - ***haven't changed***
La forme? - ***Are you okay?***
Ça peut aller - ***it's okay***
Mon cher - ***my dear***
Sinon - ***otherwise***
Harceler - ***to harass***
Veste - ***jacket***
Bruyant - ***noisy***
Efficacement - ***efficiently***
Ne s'attend - ***no one is expecting***
Trajet - ***ride***
Orphelinat - ***orphanage***
Coffre - ***trunk***
Bénévolat - ***charity work/volunteering***
S'amuser - ***to have fun***
Derrière la tête - ***in mind***
Vexes (vexer) – ***offend/hurt (to hurt)***
Un coup de main - ***some help***
Jouets - ***toys***

S'exécute (s'exécuter) - ***complies (to comply)***
Accueillir - ***to welcome***
Friandises – ***candies/sweets***
Vacarme - ***racket***
Lèvent (lever) - ***raise (to raise)***
Apercevoir - ***to notice***
Raides - ***straight***
Brun profound - ***deep brown***
Noisettes (adjective) – ***hazel***
Lumineux - ***bright***
Tablier - ***apron***
Affiche un grand sourire (afficher un grand sourire) – ***displays/shows a big smile (to show a big smile)***
Ce qui en ajoute beaucoup à son charme - ***adds a lot to her charm***
Se met à faire visiter (se mettre à) - ***begins giving them a tour of (to start/to begin)***
En chuchotant - ***by whispering***
Soudaine - ***sudden***
Manquent (manquer) - ***lack (to lack)***
S'implique - ***involves himself***
Du mieux qu'il le peut. - ***as best he can***
Bienfaiteurs - ***benefactors***
Serre (serrer) - ***holds (to hold)***
S'agenouille (s'agenouiller) - ***kneels down (to kneel down)***
Se mettre à la taille du - ***to get to the height of***
En souriant - ***while smiling***
S'étonnent (s'étonner) - ***are surprised (to be surprised)***
A souri (sourire) - ***smiled (to smile)***
Affiche une mine (afficher une mine) - ***shows a look (to show a look)***
Sereine – ***relaxed/chilled***
Que d'habitude - ***than usual***
Faire le bien - ***to do good deeds***
Tout à coup - ***all of a sudden***
N'en a pas l'air comme ça (avoir l'air) - ***may not look like it (to look/ to seem)***
Veuve - ***widow***
S'en est remise (se remettre) - ***got over it (to get over)***
Plus âgé - ***older***

Histoire 5/Story 5: L'amour sauveur

Fait figure de - ***is seen as/is thought of as (to be seen as/to be thought of as)***
Obéit presque au doigt et à l'œil (obéir) – ***obeys his almost every order (to obey)***
La perte – ***the loss***
Peines - ***sorrows***
Vient tout juste de (venir tout juste de) - ***has just (to have just)***
Met du temps (mettre du temps) - ***takes time (to take time)***
Radieux - ***radiant***
Remarque (remarquer) - ***notices (to notice)***
Fâchera (fâcher) - ***will anger (to anger)***
Je n'y arrive pas - ***I can't do it***
Cesser de vivre - ***to stop living***
Abandonner - ***to abandon/to give up on***
Vous voulez-vous en sortir? - ***Do you want to manage this situation well?***
Qui ont suivit - ***thereafter***
Enfance - ***childhood***
Reprendre goût à la vie - ***to rediscover a taste for life***
Renoue des liens (renouer les liens) - ***renews the ties (to renew the ties)***
Se familiarise - ***familiarizes (to familiarize with)***
Renoue avec des sentiments oubliés (renouer avec des sentiments oubliés) - ***reconnects with forgotten feelings (to catch up/ reconnect with forgotten feelings)***
Se laisser aller - ***to go with the flow***
Nouer des liens forts - ***to develop close ties/to build strong ties***
Sortir - ***to go out***
Demander en mariage - ***to propose***
Accueillent la nouvelle avec joie (accueillir la nouvelle) - ***greet the news with joy (to greet the news)***
Un cadre - ***a setting***
En plein air - ***outdoors***
Revenir à la vie - ***to come back to life***
C'est pour cela que - ***that is why***

L'air préféré - ***the favorite tune***
Ange sauveur - ***guardian angel***
En larmes - ***in tears***
Radieux - ***bright/radiant***
Pari fou - ***crazy bet***
Libérer de l'emprise du passé. - ***to free from the grip of the past***
Courent des jours heureux (courir des jours heureux) - ***are enjoying happy days (to enjoy happy days)***

Practice your writing:

Write a short summary of this story. Do not paraphrase.

Sample:

Cinq ans sont passés depuis qu'Arnaud a perdu l'amour de sa vie dans un terrible accident de la route. Arnaud n'arrive toujours pas à s'en remettre même après cinq années. Prisonnier du passé, rien ne lui fait oublier sa douleur.

Un soir, alors qu'Arnaud passe encore une soirée à ne rien faire., il reçoit la visite de Lisa sa petite sœur et d'Olivier son meilleur ami. Olivier est venu dans le but de faire sortir son ami. Pour ce soir, Olivier a une petite surprise pour son ami. Il l'emmène à l'orphelinat où travaille son amie Louise.

La visite de ces trois personnes fait énormément plaisir aux enfants. Un petit garçon arrive même à **arracher un sourire** à Arnaud qui n'avait pas souri depuis bien des années. En route vers la maison, Olivier avoue à Arnaud que s´ils sont allés à l'orphelinat ce soir c'est parce que Louise a aussi perdu son mari et même sa fille dans un accident de voiture.

Arracher un sourire - ***to get a smile out of/to force a smile out of***

Le lendemain, l'histoire de Louise hante les pensées d'Arnaud qui finit par repartir la voir et en discuter. Arrivé à l'orphelinat, Arnaud raconte tout à Louise qui est déjà au courant de l'histoire. Louise lui dit que c'est grâce à ses orphelins qu'elle a pu s'en sortir. La discussion se termine par Louise qui propose à Arnaud de l'aider.

Les mois suivants, Arnaud va mieux et son intérêt grandit pour Louise. Ils tombent amoureux l'un de l'autre et deviennent inséparables. Arnaud, ne voulant plus gâcher sa vie, décide de demander la main de Louise. Il l'invite à dîner un soir dans un cadre très romantique avec un dîner à la belle étoile et un violoniste. Arnaud et Louise se mettent ı danser et à l'issue de cette danse., Arnaud fait sa demande dans **es règles de l'art**. Louise accepte. Depuis, les deux âmes sœurs ›assent leur temps dans l'orphelinat.

À l'issue - ***at the end***
_es règles de l'art - ***the proper way***
Âmes sœurs - ***soulmates***

Histoire 6/Story 6: Un anniversaire

Héloïse réfléchit à comment **fêter** l'anniversaire de sa meilleure amie Sophie. Les deux filles sont amies depuis leur **enfance**, donc Héloïse **veut bien faire les choses** pour le 25ème anniversaire de Sophie. Avec le budget qu'elle **a prévu,** elle ne pourra pas organiser une fête dans un club. Ça lui couterait trop **cher**. Une fête surprise chez Sophie n'est pas non plus envisageable. Elle **s'**en **rendrait compte** très facilement. L'idée la plus raisonnable semble être une belle sortie au restaurant qui serait quand même une surprise pour Sophie.

Fêter - ***to celebrate***
Enfance - ***childhood***
Veut bien faire les choses (faire bien les choses) - ***wants to do things***

right (to do things right)
A prévu (prévoir) - ***planned (to plan)***
Cher - ***expensive***
Rendrait compte (se rendre compte) - ***would realize (to realize)***

Héloïse s'occupe par la suite **d'avertir** les amis et la famille de Sophie. Elle invite ses parents, son frère et sa sœur. D'autres amis sont aussi **prévenus**. **Le mot d'ordre** est qu´elle doit **croire** que tout le monde **a oublié** son anniversaire. La surprise **se met rapidement en place**. Après quelques recherches, la jeune femme choisit *La Tour d'Or*, qui est le restaurant préféré de Sophie. Elle **se déplace** au restaurant pour faire les réservations et tout expliquer au personnel « Bonjour ! **J'ai besoin de** parler au **gérant du restaurant.**

Avertir - ***to inform***
Prévenus - ***informed***
Le mot d'ordre - ***the motto***
Croire - ***to believe***
A oublié (oublier) - ***has forgotten (to forget)***
Se met rapidement en place - ***is quickly put in place/is quickly set up***
Se déplace (se déplacer) - ***moves (to move)***
J'ai besoin de - ***I need to***
Gérant du restaurant - ***the restaurant manager***

- Bonjour Madame! **Veuillez patienter**. Je vais le chercher. Asseyez-vous.
- Merci Monsieur!"

Veuillez patienter - ***Please wait***

Quelques minutes plus tard le gérant arrive et **s'adresse à** Héloïse: "Bonjour Madame! Bienvenue à *la Tour d'Or*. Que puis-je faire pour vous?

- Bonjour! Je viens pour réserver.
- Mais vous auriez pu vous éviter le **dérangement** et faire vos réservations par téléphone.
- Oui je sais bien, mais c'est un peu particulier.

- Ah bon?! **Racontez-moi tout ça.**
- C'est l'anniversaire de ma meilleure amie et je veux lui organiser une petite **fête surprise** chez vous.
- Je vois. Ce sera pour quand?
- Vendredi prochain. C'est possible en **soirée?**
- Oui ! **Parfaitement**. Combien de personnes?
- Nous serons 18. Je pense que trois tables nous **suffiront.**
- Vous avez raison. Patientez un moment, je vous apporte notre menu. Vous allez pouvoir faire votre choix pour votre fête.
- D'accord. Je vous remercie."

S'adresse à - ***speaks to***
Éviter - ***to avoid***
Dérangement - ***inconvenience***
Racontez-moi tout ça - ***Tell me the whole story***
Fête surprise - ***surprise party***
Soirée - ***evening***
Parfaitement - ***absolutely***
Suffiront - ***will be enough/will suffice***

Pendant que le gérant s'occupe d'apporter les menus. Héloïse **explique au reste du personnel** le **déroulement** de la surprise. Héloïse veut que leurs tables soient un peu éloignées de l'entrée. La surprise doit être parfaite. Une dizaine de minutes plus tard, le gérant revient avec le menu du restaurant et un catalogue des gâteaux d'anniversaire: "Voilà le menu. Vous voulez du poulet, de la viande, ou du poisson en plat principal?

Explique au reste du personnel - ***explains to the rest of the staff***
Éloignées - ***far***

- Non! En fait, j'ai déjà **une petite idée** sur vos plats. Avec mon amie, on est des habituées de votre restaurant. Pour cette fête je voudrais des **crevettes** et d'autres fruits de mer en **assortiment**. Avec quelques **légumes en sauce** en **accompagnement**. C'est possible?
- Oui c'est **tout à fait faisable**. Et en **entrée**? Du **potage** ou bien une salade?

- Vu que nous aurons du gâteau, une salade **serait préférable**. Je vous laisse le choix de la salade. Je sais que je peux vous **faire confiance**.
- Vous avez une préférence concernant les boissons? Des vins **en tête**?
- Non ! Pas vraiment. **Je compte sur vous** pour choisir **ce qui va avec** nos plats.
- D'accord Madame. Passons au gâteau. Voilà ce que nous proposons.
- **Ce n'est pas la peine**. Mon amie aime tout ce qui contient du chocolat, de la crème et des fraises.
- Et bien parfait."

Une petite idée - ***an idea***
Crevettes - ***shrimps***
Assortiment - ***assortment***
Légumes en sauce - ***vegetables in sauce***
Accompagnement - ***side order***
Tout à fait faisable - ***quite doable***
Entrée - ***first course***
Potage - ***soup***
Serait préférable - ***would be preferred***
Faire confiance - ***to trust***
En tête - ***in mind***
Je compte sur vous - ***I'm counting on you***
Ce qui va avec - ***what goes with it***
Ce n'est pas la peine - ***It is not necessary***

Après le restaurant, la **prochaine étape** pour Héloïse est de trouver une excuse pour attirer Sophie au restaurant. **Ayant** du **mal à trouver** un moyen de le faire, elle décide de **laisser ça** pour le soir même. Elle lui trouvera une raison pour **l'attirer** à la *Tour d'Or.* Héloïse a donc tout réglé pour l'anniversaire.

Prochaine étape - ***next step***
Ayant du mal à trouver - ***having trouble finding***
Laisser ça – ***to leave it***
Attirer - ***to attract***

Le jour de l'anniversaire arrive très vite. Sophie est toute **triste.** Personne n'a pensé à son anniversaire. Elle pense que tout le monde l'a oublié. Héloïse fait croire à son amie qu'elle avait un rendez-vous avec un homme. Durant la soirée, elle appelle Sophie au téléphone pour lui faire croire qu'elle a un problème. Elle lui demande de lui **venir en aide.** Sophie va vite au restaurant **au secours de son amie**.

Triste - ***sad***
Venir - ***to come***
Aide - ***help***
Venir en aide - ***to come to assist/to come to help***
Au secours de son amie - ***to the rescue of her friend***

Arrivée sur les lieux, Sophie entre vite pour y chercher son amie. Là, elle est surprise d'y trouver tous ses **proches** lui criant "Surprise!" Elle **comprend** que son amie n'a rien et qu'elle lui a juste fait une surprise pour son anniversaire: "Héloïse! Tu as quand même pensé à moi.

- Heureusement! **Les amis c'est fait pour ça.**"
- Sophie prend place et la fête peut commencer.

Arrivée sur les lieux - ***present on site/once present on the scene***
Proches - ***relatives***
Comprend - ***understands***
Les amis c'est fait pour ça – ***that's what friends are for***

Le gérant du restaurant **vient en personne souhaiter** un bon anniversaire à Sophie. Il se met ensuite à présenter le menu de la soirée: "Bienvenue à *La Tour d'Or*. Pour le diner de ce soir, Nous avons mis en place avec l'aide d'Héloïse un menu **aux goûts de** Sophie. En entrée nous **avons prévu** une salade landaise composée de laitue, d'asperges, de **maïs,** de **pignons de pin**, de tomates, de **tranches de foie gras de canard,** de **jambon,** de **magret de canard fumé** et de **gésiers de canard** pour en faire une landaise authentique. Par la suite viendra un assortiment de fruits de mer accompagné de légumes sautés. Pour le dessert, nous avons élaboré un gâteau unique. Les directives d'Héloïse nous ont beaucoup aidées. Nous sommes parvenus à faire un gâteau aux **goûts** de Sophie. Mais ça reste une surprise qu'on laisse pour plus tard. Passez une bonne soirée."

Tout le monde à l'air de bien **apprécier**. Héloïse est félicitée pour son organisation de la fête.
Vient en personne - ***comes in person***
Souhaiter **- to wish**
Aux goûts de - ***to the taste of***
Avons prévu - ***have planned***
Maïs - ***corn***
Pignons de pin - ***pine nuts***
Tranches de foie gras de canard - ***slices of foie gras***
Jambon - ***ham***
Magret de canard fumé - ***smoked duck breast***
Gésiers de canard - ***duck gizzards***
Élaboré - ***created***
Goûts - ***tastes***
Apprécier - ***to appreciate***

L'entrée ne **met** pas beaucoup de **temps (mettre du temps)** à arriver. Une salade landaise pour commencer ce repas d'anniversaire. Du vin vient **s´ajouter** au plat. Couteaux et fourchettes en main, les invités dégustent la salade qui **passe toute seule.** Cette entrée **remporte un franc succès**. Tout le monde **complimente** le chef. Il se déplace en personne aux tables **des convives**. Il tient à **souhaiter** un bon anniversaire à Sophie.

Met - ***puts***
Temps - ***time***
Mettre du temps - ***to take some time***
S´ajouter - ***to be added***
Passe toute seule - ***goes alone***
Remporte un franc succès - ***is a great success***
Complimente - ***compliment***
Des convives - ***the guests***

Après avoir **débarrassé** la table et **mis** de **nouveaux couverts**, **les serveurs** apportent la **suite,** de fabuleux assortiments de fruits de mer : **du crabe, des crevettes, des langoustes, des moules** et même du **homard** composent **ces plateaux.** Des légumes sautés accompagnent les fruits de mer. Cette fois c'est du **vin blanc** que le gérant a choisi pour venir compléter cet **assortiment**. Sophie, Héloïse et leurs invités **se régalent** du repas. **Hélas,** même avec tous ces efforts, il y a toujours quelqu'un **qui trouve à redire**. Mélanie, la grande sœur de Sophie, dit **qu'elle trouve que** pour des fruits de mer ce n'est pas **assez épicé**. Cela **fâche** un peu le gérant qui **s'est donné beaucoup de mal.** Malgré cela, il demande **quand même** à ce qu'on lui apporte de la **sauce épicée** qu'il y a en cuisine. Comme ça, tout le monde est satisfait. Le repas se termine **en moins de temps qu'il ne faut pour le dire** et il ne reste plus aucun fruit de mer sur les plateaux.

Débarrassé - ***cleared***
Mis - ***put***
Nouveaux couverts - ***new flatware***
Les serveurs - ***the servers***
La suite - ***the rest***
Du crabe - ***crab***
Des crevettes - ***shrimps***
Des langoustes - ***lobsters***
Des moules - ***mussels***
Homard - ***lobster***
Ces plateaux - ***these platters***
Vin blanc - ***white wine***
Assortiment - ***assortment***
Se régalent (se régaler) - ***feast on (to feast on)***
Hélas - ***unfortunately***
Qui trouve à redire - ***who finds fault***
Elle trouve que - ***she finds that***
Assez épicé - ***spicy enough***
Fâche - ***gets upset***
S'est donné beaucoup de mal - ***has worked hard***
Quand même - ***still***
Sauce épicée - ***hot sauce***
En moins de temps qu'il ne faut pour le dire - ***in no time***

Héloïse est satisfaite et se dit que tout s**e passe bien** pour son amie. Elle **se retire** du reste du groupe pour parler au gérant: "Pour le gâteau, vous allez attendre que **je vous fasse signe**. On passe d'abord à l'**ouverture** des **cadeaux.**

Se passe bien - ***is going well***
Se retire - ***retreats***
Je vous fasse signe - ***I signal to you***
L'ouverture - ***the opening***
Cadeaux - ***gifts***

- **C'est comme vous voulez** Madame. J'espère que notre travail **vous convient.**
- Oui ! Tout le monde **s'amuse.** Sophie **est aux anges.**
- Je vous remercie.
- Il n'y a pas de quoi. Merci à vous."

C'est comme vous voulez - ***it is how you like it***
Vous convient - ***suits you***
S'amuse - ***is having fun***
Est aux anges - ***is ecstatic***

Héloïse retourne à table. En **parfaite organisatrice,** elle **annonce la suite des événements.** "C'est le moment de donner ses cadeaux à Sophie! Tiens voilà **le mien**.

- Merci! Qu'est-ce que c'est?
- Vas-y, ouvre-le !
- Oh! C'est le **parfum** que je voulais m'offrir. Merci Héloïse. C'est tellement gentil de ta part.
- Mais de rien. Allez tout le monde, donnez-lui vos cadeaux."

Sophie, toute contente, **reçoit** beaucoup de cadeaux. Elle les ouvre **les uns après les autres**: des bijoux, des vêtements, des accessoires et quelques **produits cosmétiques**. La jeune femme est très **heureuse**.

Parfaite organisatrice - ***perfect organizer***
Annonce la suite des événements - ***announces the following events***
Le mien - ***mine***

Parfum - ***perfume***
Reçoit - ***receives***
Produits cosmétiques - ***cosmetic products***
Heureuse - ***pleased***

Après l'ouverture des cadeaux, c'est le moment du gâteau. Héloïse fait signe au personnel du restaurant pour qu'ils apportent le gâteau. Quelques secondes plus tard un **chariot** portant un **magnifique** gâteau arrive. Il est **orné** de 25 **bougies**. Tout le monde **se met aussitôt** à chanter "Joyeux anniversaire, joyeux anniversaire." Sophie est **ravie.** "**Souffle** les bougies! Mais **d'abord fais un vœu**." Lui dit son amie. "Oui!" RépondSophie. Elle fait son vœu et souffle les bougies de son gâteau.

Chariot - ***trolley***
Magnifique - ***wonderful***
Orné - ***decorated***
Bougies - ***candles***
Se met à - ***begins to***
Ravie - ***delighted***
Souffle - ***blows***
D'abord fais un vœu - ***first make a wish***

Le **maître des lieux** revient vers eux pour leur présenter le gâteau: "voici un gâteau que nous avons conçu spécialement pour Sophie. Nous **avons pris en compte** ce qu'elle aimait et nous **avons opté** pour un gâteau au chocolat et à la fraise **façon forêt noire**.

Maître des lieux - ***owner (master of the house/place)***
Avons pris en compte - ***taken into account***
Avons opté - ***opted***
Façon forêt noire - ***black forest (name of cake) style***

- Merci Monsieur.
- Je vous en prie Madame. Alors, entre chaque couche de gâteau il y a de la crème chantilly à la fraise. Le tout est **recouvert** d'une crème à la vanille **parsemée** de **copeaux** de chocolats et **garni** de **morceaux** de fraises.

- Très bien ! Où est le couteau ? J'**ai hâte** d'y goûter.
- Le voilà Madame. Nous allons vous chercher des petites assiettes et **de quoi servir.**"

Recouvert - ***covered***
Parsemée - ***sprinkled***
Copeaux - ***chocolate sprinkles***
Garni - ***filled***
Morceaux - ***pieces***
J'ai hâte ***I can't wait***
De quoi servir - ***something to serve with***

Les couverts arrivent et le gérant revient avec un **seau portant** une bouteille de champagne: "Voilà de quoi bien accompagner votre gâteau. **C'est offert par la maison.** Bon anniversaire Madame.

- Merci c'est si gentil de votre part. Joignez-vous à nous."

Les couverts - ***the cutlery***
Seau – **bucket**
Portant - **carrying**
C'est offert par la maison - ***it is on the house***

Héloïse qui **s'est occupée** de couper le gâteau, apporte une **part** au gérant qui la remercie. Tout le monde apprécie le bon gâteau.

Héloïse a **réussi son pari** et elle a organisé une superbe fête pour son amie. Le repas d'anniversaire se **termine dans la joie**.

S'est occupée - ***took care***
Part - ***piece***
Réussi son pari - ***achieved her goal (won her bet)***
Termine dans la joie - ***ends in joy***

Héloïse propose à son amie de l'accompagner chez elle pour l'aider à porter tous ses cadeaux. Sophie est contente. Les deux amies remercient les invités et les **raccompagnent** avant de **s'en aller** elles-mêmes. Un serveur vient et leur tend des paquets: "Madame. Vous oubliez les restes du gâteau.

- **Les restes** du gâteau?!
- Oui il en reste. Ce **serait dommage** de les **gâcher**.
- Oui mais justement ça ne sera pas du **gâchis**. **Reprenez-les** et mangez ce qui reste du gâteau avec vos collègues.
- Oh ! Merci infiniment Madame.
- Je vous en prie."

Raccompagnent - ***see them to the door***
S'en aller - ***to leave***
Les restes - ***the leftovers***
Serait dommage - ***would be too bad/a shame***
Gâcher - ***to waste***
Gâchis –***waste***
Reprenez-les - ***take them back***

Sophie regarde son amie d'**un air étonné** et lui dit: "Depuis quand tu laisses du gâteau toi?"

- Depuis qu'on a ces sacs **remplis** de cadeaux à porter. Nous n'avons pas de troisièmes bras pour porter plus de paquets.
- Je vois. Ça m'avait étonnée.
- Oui. En plus **vu que** tu es une habituée, ces bonnes actions te **favoriseront** par rapport aux autres clients. Tu auras sûrement des **trucs offerts.**
- Je vois que tu **penses à tout toi.**"

Un air étonné - ***a bewildered look***
Remplis - ***full***
Vu que - ***since***
Favoriseront - ***will favor***
Trucs offerts - ***things offered***
Penses à tout toi - ***you think of everything***

Sur le chemin, vers la station du métro, Héloïse et Sophie discutent de la soirée: "Héloïse. C'est si gentil de ta part d'avoir fait tout ça. Je pensais que tout le monde m'avait oubliée.

- C'était **fait exprès.** J'ai demandé à tout le monde de **jouer le jeu.** C'était une belle surprise, non?
- Ça pour une surprise, **s'en était une**. J'ai vraiment pensé que tu avais un problème.
- Pardon pour ça!
- Ce n'est pas grave. Merci beaucoup. C'était magnifique. Sûrement le meilleur anniversaire que j'ai eu.
- Mais de rien, rien n'est trop beau pour toi."

Fait exprès - ***on purpose***
Jouer le jeu - ***to play along***
S'en était une - ***it was one***

Elles prennent ensuite le métro et partent chez Sophie. Arrivées chez celle-ci, comme il **se fait tard**, elle invite Héloïse à passer la nuit chez elle. Vu que le lendemain est un samedi, Héloïse accepte l'invitation. Et ainsi se termine cette soirée d'anniversaire.

Il se fait tard - ***it's getting late***

Vocabulary Recap 6

Fêter - ***to celebrate***
Enfance - ***childhood***
Veut bien faire les choses (faire bien les choses) - ***wants to do things right (to do things right)***
A prévu (prévoir) - ***planned (to plan)***
Cher - ***expensive***
Rendrait compte (se rendre compte) - ***would realize (to realize)***
Avertir - ***to inform***
Prévenus - ***informed***
Le mot d'ordre - ***the motto***
Croire - ***to believe***
A oublié (oublier) - ***has forgotten (to forget)***
Se met rapidement en place - ***is quickly put in place/is quickly set up***
Se déplace (se déplacer) - ***moves (to move)***
J'ai besoin de - ***I need to***
Gérant du restaurant - ***the restaurant manager***
Veuillez patienter - ***Please wait***
S'adresse à - ***speaks to***
Éviter - ***to avoid***
Dérangement - ***inconvenience***
Racontez-moi tout ça - ***Tell me the whole story***
Fête surprise - ***surprise party***
Soirée - ***evening***
Parfaitement - ***absolutely***
Suffiront - ***will be enough/will suffice***
Explique au reste du personnel - ***explains to the rest of the staff***
Éloignées - ***far***
Une petite idée - ***an idea***
Crevettes - ***shrimps***
Assortiment - ***assortment***
Légumes en sauce - ***vegetables in sauce***
Accompagnement - ***side order***
Tout à fait faisable - ***quite doable***
Entrée - ***first course***
Potage - ***soup***

Histoire 6/Story 6: Un anniversaire

Serait préférable - ***would be preferred***
Faire confiance - ***to trust***
En tête - ***in mind***
Je compte sur vous - ***I'm counting on you***
Ce qui va avec - ***what goes with it***
Ce n'est pas la peine - ***It is not necessary***
Prochaine étape - ***next step***
Ayant du mal à trouver - ***having trouble finding***
Laisser ça - ***to leave it***
Attirer - ***to attract***
Triste - ***sad***
Venir - ***to come***
Aide - ***help***
Venir en aide - ***to come to assist/to come to help***
Au secours de son amie - ***to the rescue of her friend***
Arrivée sur les lieux - ***present on site/once present on the scene***
Proches - ***relatives***
Comprend - ***understands***
Les amis c'est fait pour ça - ***that's what friends are for***
Vient en personne - ***comes in person***
Souhaiter **- to wish**
Aux goûts de - ***to the taste of***
Avons prévu - ***have planned***
Maïs - ***corn***
Pignons de pin - ***pine nuts***
Tranches de foie gras de canard - ***slices of foie gras***
Jambon - ***ham***
Magret de canard fumé - ***smoked duck breast***
Gésiers de canard - ***duck gizzards***
Élaboré - ***created***
Goûts - ***tastes***
Apprécier - ***to appreciate***
Met - ***puts***
Temps - ***time***
Mettre du temps- ***to take some time***
S´ajouter - ***to be added***
Passe toute seule - ***goes alone***
Remporte un franc succès - ***is a great success***

Complimente - ***compliment***
Des convives - ***the guests***
Débarrassé - ***cleared***
Mis - ***put***
Nouveaux couverts - ***new flatware***
Les serveurs - ***the servers***
La suite - ***the rest***
Du crabe - ***crab***
Des crevettes - ***shrimps***
Des langoustes - ***lobsters***
Des moules - ***mussels***
Homard - ***lobster***
Ces plateaux - ***these platters***
Vin blanc - ***white wine***
Assortiment - ***assortment***
Se régalent (se régaler) - ***feast on (to feast on)***
Hélas - ***unfortunately***
Qui trouve à redire - ***who finds fault***
Elle trouve que - ***she finds that***
Assez épicé - ***spicy enough***
Fâche - ***gets upset***
S'est donné beaucoup de mal - ***has worked hard***
Quand même - ***still***
Sauce épicée - ***hot sauce***
En moins de temps qu'il ne faut pour le dire - ***in no time***
Se passe bien - ***is going well***
Se retire - ***retreats***
Je vous fasse signe - ***I signal to you***
L'ouverture - ***the opening***
Cadeaux - ***gifts***
C'est comme vous voulez - ***it is how you like it***
Vous convient - ***suit you***
S'amuse - ***is having fun***
Est aux anges - ***is ecstatic***
Parfaite organisatrice - ***perfect organizer***
Annonce la suite des événements - ***announces the following events***
Le mien - ***mine***
Parfum - ***perfume***

Histoire 6/Story 6: Un anniversaire

Reçoit - ***receives***
Produits cosmétiques - ***cosmetic products***
Heureuse - ***pleased***
Chariot - ***trolley***
Magnifique - ***wonderful***
Orné - ***decorated***
Bougies - ***candles***
Se met à - ***begins to***
Ravie - ***delighted***
Souffle - ***blows***
D'abord fais un vœu - ***first make a wish***
Maître des lieux - ***owner (master of the house/place)***
Avons pris en compte - ***taken into account***
Avons opté - ***opted***
Façon forêt noire - ***black forest (name of cake) style***
Recouvert - ***covered***
Parsemée - ***sprinkled***
Copeaux de chocolat - ***chocolate sprinkles***
Garni - ***filled***
Morceaux - ***pieces***
J'ai hâte ***I can't wait***
De quoi servir - ***something to serve with***
Les couverts - ***the cutlery***
Seau – **bucket**
Portant - **carrying**
C'est offert par la maison - ***it is on the house***
S'est occupée - ***took care***
Part - ***piece***
Réussi son pari - ***achieved her goal (won her bet)***
Termine dans la joie - ***ends in joy***
Raccompagnent - ***see them to the door***
S'en aller - ***to leave***
Les restes - ***the leftovers***
Serait dommage - ***would be too bad/a shame***
Gâcher - ***to waste***
Gâchis –***waste***
Reprenez-les - ***take them back***
Un air étonné - ***a bewildered look***

Remplis - ***full***
Vu que - ***since***
Favoriseront - ***will favor***
Trucs offerts - ***things offered***
Penses à tout toi - ***you think of everything***
Fait exprès - ***on purpose***
Jouer le jeu - ***to play along***
C'en était une - ***it was one***
Il se fait tard - ***it's getting late***

Practice your writing:

Write a short summary of this story. Do not paraphrase.

Sample:

Pour l'anniversaire de sa meilleure amie, Héloïse pense à organise une fête à *La Tour d'Or,* le restaurant préféré de Sophie sa meilleur amie. Elle contacte tout le monde pour les prévenir de la surprise.

Héloïse se déplace au restaurant. Elle y fait les réservations e prépare tout avec le gérant du restaurant. Elle fait part des **goûts personnels** de Sophie au gérant.

Goûts personnels - ***personal tastes***

Le jour de son anniversaire ,Sophie pense que tout le monde l'a oubliée. Personne ne lui souhaite un bon anniversaire. Héloïse lu fait croire qu'elle doit sortir avec un homme au restaurant. Le soi même Sophie reçoit **un coup de fil** de son amie qui lui dit qu'elle a u problème et qu'elle a besoin de son aide. Sophie court voir son ami au restaurant mais elle découvre cette belle surprise.

Un coup de fil - ***a phone call***

Une salade landaise est prévue en entrée à laquelle vient s'ajoute du bon vin rouge. La salade est suivie d'un fabuleux assortiment d fruits de mer accompagné de légumes sautés. Après ce plat, Héloïs prend l'initiative de proposer d'ouvrir les cadeaux avant de passer a gâteau. Tout le monde approuve et Sophie aime tous ses cadeaux.

Après l'ouverture des cadeaux **vient le tour** du gâteau. Une grand **génoise** au chocolat et à la fraise comme l'aime Sophie. Une bouteill de champagne offerte par le restaurant vient compléter l'ensemble.

'ient le tour du - ***comes the turn of***
;énoise - ***sponge cake***

La fête se termine dans les meilleures conditions. Et les deux amies ɜntrent ensemble chez Sophie pour y passer la nuit.

Histoire 7/Story 7: Une soirée au cinéma

Les choses ont beaucoup évolué pour Robin depuis **sa venue** dans son nouveau lycée. Il s'est fait beaucoup d'amis et **est devenu** très populaire. Les choses **semblent aller pour le mieux** aussi entre lui et la belle Sandrine. Le jeune garçon a de vrais sentiments pour elle. Il envisage de les lui avouer mais il n'**ose** pas encore le faire. **Profitant** d'une discussion avec son ami Jean, il lui demande des **conseils**: "Dis-moi Jean. Toi, tu as beaucoup de succès auprès des filles. Comment tu fais pour les inviter à **sortir avec toi**?

Sa venue - ***his arrival***
Est devenu - ***has become***
Semblent aller pour le mieux - ***seem to be fine***
Profitant - ***taking advantage of***
Conseils - ***advice***
Sortir avec toi - ***to go out with you***

- Eh Bien! Il n'y a pas de secret pour ça. Tu vas la voir et tu lui demandes.
- Ce n'est pas aussi simple! Surtout quand il s'agit d'une bonne amie à toi.
- Bonne amie?! Tu es **amoureux** de Sandrine?
- Je **n'irai pas jusqu'à dire** que je suis **fou d'elle**, mais y a quelque chose de particulier. C'est une fille assez **mignonne** et **sympa**. Elle est aussi la première à m'avoir parlé quand je suis arrivé ici.
- **Allez, avoue** que tu l'aimes!
- Oui bon! C'est vrai. Je l'aime et j'aimerai l'inviter à sortir pour le lui dire. Je ne sais ni comment le faire ni où **l'emmener.**
- Tu n'as qu'à l'inviter chez toi pour voir un film et tu lui diras que tu l'aimes. Elle **a l'habitude** de venir chez toi non?
- Oui **certes**, mais c'était pour réviser et non lui **avouer** mes **sentiments.**
- Tu n'as qu'à reprendre mon idée, l'inviter au cinéma pour voir un film romantique, puis vous **promener** au parc qui est à côté. Là, tu lui avoueras tout.
- **En voilà** une bonne idée ! Je vais le lui dire après les cours."

Amoureux - ***in love***
N'irai pas jusqu'à dire - ***I wouldn't say that***
Fou d'elle - ***crazy about her***
Mignonne - ***cute***
Sympa - ***nice***
Allez, avoue - ***Come on, admit***
L'emmener - ***to take her***
A l'habitude - ***used to***
Certes - ***certainly***
Avouer - ***to confess***
Sentiments - ***feelings***
Vous promener (se promener) - ***to take a walk***
En voilà - ***and here is***

La journée au lycée **se poursuit normalement**. À la **fin** des **cours**, Robin est avec Sandrine et il lui parle de ses projets pour le week-end. "Dis-moi Sandrine, tu fais quoi ce week-end?

- Je n'ai rien de prévu. Pourquoi?!
- **Ben** si tu n'as rien à faire, qu'est-ce que tu penses de sortir avec moi?
- Sortir avec toi?!
- Oui, j'ai envie d'aller au cinéma. Tu ne veux pas venir avec moi?
- Si si! Je veux bien. Ça va être super.
- Ah! Génial. On y va samedi soir?
- Oui, c'est parfait. On va **se mettre d'accord** sur l'heure demain? **Je dois y aller** maintenant, à demain!
- À **plus** Sandrine!"

Se poursuit normalement - ***continues as normal/normally***
Fin - ***end***
Cours - ***classes***
Ben - ***well***
Se mettre d'accord - ***to make a decision/to decide***
Je dois y aller - ***I have got to go/I must go***
À plus! - ***see you!***

Robin, **aux anges** pour son premier rendez-vous, court rentrer chez lui.

Une fois **chez lui**, Robin prend son ordinateur. Il y cherche les films que proposent les salles de cinéma de la ville pour samedi. Comme il **a en tête** de voir un film romantique avec Sandrine, les recherches lui sont très facilitées. Le jeune homme trouve facilement une salle qui propose un film à la fois romantique et dramatique. Maintenant, Robin a toutes les informations qu'il lui faut, pour proposer **concrètement** à Sandrine une soirée au cinéma avec lui.

Aux anges - ***thrilled***
Chez lui - ***at his place***
A en tête - ***has in mind***
Concrètement - ***concretely***

Le lendemain matin, Robin va voir Sandrine. Il lui parle de ses **trouvailles** de la veille: Bonjour Sandrine.

Histoire 7/Story 7: Une soirée au cinéma

- Bonjour Robin. Ça va?
- Ouais ça va merci, et toi?
- Je vais bien aussi, merci. Alors? le cinéma?
- Oui, justement. Hier soir, j'ai fait quelques petites recherches sur internet. **Ils passent** **"**Le temps d'un automne" au Louxor, samedi soir.
- Super! J'ai toujours adoré ce film. Mandy Moore est l'une de mes actrices préférées. Quand le film est sorti, c'était une grande **vedette.** Je suis ravie de le voir sur le grand écran ça sera la toute première fois.
- Mandy Moore, c'est l'**interprète** du **premier rôle féminin,** n'est-ce pas?
- Oui, sa chanson dans le film est tellement belle ! C'est la scène que je préfère dans le film. La séance est pour quelle heure?
- **Tant mieux alors**. Le film commence à 20h50. Je **passe te chercher** à 20h30? Je vais prendre la voiture de mon père.
- Oui, c'est d'accord. **Vite!** Allons en cours maintenant."

Les deux **adolescents** partent en classe. La journée de cours se passe **le plus normalement du monde** et la semaine se finit très vite.

Trouvailles - ***findings***
Ils passent - ***they are showing***
Vedette - ***star***
Écran - ***screen***
L'interprète - ***the performer***
Premier rôle féminin - ***leading actress***
Tant mieux alors - ***then all the better***
Passe te chercher - ***going to/will pick you up***
Vite – ***quickly***
Adolescents - ***teenagers***
Le plus normalement du monde - ***as usual***

Samedi arrive très rapidement. Robin est **tout excité à l'idée de** sortir avec la fille qu'il aime. Le soir même, il passe même beaucoup de temps à se choisir une **tenue adéquate** pour l'occasion. Après une longue **séance d'essayage,** il arrive enfin à se décider. Il opte pour une tenue **classe et décontractée**, de quoi séduire la **charmante** Sandrine.

L'heure du rendez-vous approche et Robin devient de plus en plus nerveux. À 20h, il prend la voiture de son père et part chercher Sandrine Arrivé là-bas, il trouve Sandrine en train de l'attendre sur **le pas de la porte**. Robin la **klaxonne** et elle monte en voiture. Le jeune homme discute avec elle avant de **reprendre la route**:

"Bonsoir Sandrine. Tues **très en beauté** ce soir.

- Bonsoir. Merci. Toi aussi tu es particulièrement beau ce soir.
- C'est gentil, merci . On y va?
- Oui!"

Tout excité à l'idée - ***all excited about***
Tenue adéquate - ***appropriate clothing/suitable outfit***
Séance d'essayage - ***fitting session***
Classe et décontractée - ***classy and relaxed***
Charmante - ***charming***
Pas de la porte - ***doorstep***
Klaxonne – ***honks/beeps***
Reprendre la route - ***to hit the road again***
Très en beauté - ***very beautiful/stunning***

Et la voiture **redémarre**. Arrivés au cinéma, ils sont surpris de voir qu'il n y a pas **beaucoup de monde**. Cela **met** Robin vraiment plus à l'aise (mettre à l'aise). Il se dit que ça ne sera pas difficile d'**avouer ses sentiments** à Sandrine. Robin va acheter les billets, du popcorn et des sodas. Ils **prennent place (prendre place) par la suite**. **L'employé du cinéma/ le surveillant** passe vérifier les **billets** des **spectateurs** et avant le **début de la séance** Robin essaye de discuter un peu avec **sa belle**:

"J'espère que tu aimes le popcorn et le soda, sinon je vais aller te chercher autre chose.

Redémarre - ***restarts***
Beaucoup de monde - ***many people***
Met - ***puts***
À l'aise - ***comfortable/at ease***

Histoire 7/Story 7: Une soirée au cinéma

Mettre à l'aise - ***to put at ease***
Avouer ses sentiments - ***to confess his feelings***
Prennent place par la suite – ***then they take their places***
Prendre place - ***to sit***
L'ouvreur - ***the usher***
Vérifier - ***to check/to verify***
Billets - ***tickets***
Spectateurs – ***audience/spectators***
Début de la séance - ***beginning of the session***
Sa belle - ***his beauty***

- **Ce n'est pas la peine**. C'est **parfait**.
- Très bien alors. Dis, tu savais que ce film est en fait **une adaptation** d'un livre ?
- Oui **je l'ai lu.** Comme je **l'ai lu** après avoir vu le film, c'était plus facile d'imaginer les personnages. En fait, ce n'est pas vraiment une adaptation mais le **réalisateur** et le **scénariste** du film se sont inspirés du livre. Les Américains sont vraiment doués pour ça.
- Je vois. Honnêtement ,toi ,tu préfères le livre ou le film? Beaucoup préfèrent les films à la lecture.
- **Franchement** j'aime les deux, et toi tu préfères quoi?
- Aucun! J'aime les deux aussi. Que ce soit la littérature ou le cinéma, les deux sont des arts époustouflants. Ils **se complètent**, on voit des adaptations de l'un vers l'autre.
- Super. C'est la première fois que je viens au Louxor. **La plupart du temps** on va à La Bastille avec ma famille.
- C'est la première fois pour moi aussi. C'est une assez belle salle je trouve. Elle est très grande, **mais il** n'y a pas beaucoup de monde ce soir.
- Oui, je préfère. On pourra bien apprécier le film comme ça."

Ce n'est pas la peine - ***It is not worth it***
Parfait - ***perfect***
Une adaptation - ***an adaptation***
Je l'ai lu - ***I have read it***
Réalisateur - ***director***
Scénariste - ***scriptwriter***

Franchement – ***honestly/frankly***
Époustouflants – ***breathtaking/mind-blowing***
Se complètent - ***complete one another***
La plupart du temps - ***most of the time***

Leur discussion est **interrompue** par le début du film. Le film est très riche en émotions. Les minutes **passent par dizaines** sans se faire ressentir. Sandrine est très **prise par le film**. Elle ne prête pas beaucoup d'attention au pauvre Robin. Il **en désespérerait** sûrement s'il n'était pas lui aussi absorbé par le film. La **fameuse scène** de la chanson arrive enfin. Sandrine, **prise d'émotion** lors de cette scène, prend la main de Robin. Le jeune homme est **tout à coup ramené à la réalité** et il **serre la main** de sa voisine. Le film continue et son **déroulement** inspire Robin et touche énormément la jeune Sandrine.

Interrompue - ***interrupted***
Passent par dizaines - ***pass quickly***
Prise par le film - ***taken by the film/concentrated on the film***
Désespérerait - ***would have lost hope***
Fameuse scène - ***famous scene***
Prise d'émotion - ***feeling emotional/moved***
Tout à coup ramené à la réalité - ***suddenly brought back to reality***
Serre la main - ***holds her hand tightly***
Déroulement - ***progress***

Le film terminé, Robin demande à Sandrine ses réactions sur le film:

"Alors, tu as aimé le voir sur grand écran?

- Oui, c'était **merveilleux**. Ça me touche vraiment beaucoup ce genre d'histoire. Merci Robin pour ce film.
- De rien. On en fera d'autres encore comme ça, si tu veux.
- Oui, **j'en serai vraiment ravie**.
- Les décors sont magnifiques. Ces paysages d'Amérique profonde sont très **propices** à ce genre d'histoire. J'aime également l'évolution des **personnages** le long du film.

- Moi aussi. Tout est vraiment parfait dans ce film. Les décors, le scénario, les acteurs, les **figurants**, **le maquillage, l'éclairage** tout, mais vraiment tout y est parfait !
- Haha! Je vois que tu l'aimes beaucoup. Bon on y va maintenant?
- D'accord, allons-y."

Merveilleux - ***wonderful***
J'en serai vraiment ravie - ***I will be so delighted to***
Propices - ***suitable***
Personnages - ***characters***
Figurants - ***extras (for a movie)***
Le maquillage - ***the makeup***
L'éclairage - ***the lighting***

À la sortie du cinéma, comme il n'était pas très tard, Robin propose à Sandrine d'aller **faire un tour** dans le parc qui n'était pas loin. La jeune fille accepte. Elle, qui aime les **promenades nocturnes**, ne pouvait refuser. Ce soir-là, il fait assez **doux** et le ciel est bien **clair**, ça leur permettra de bien voir les étoiles.

Faire un tour - ***to go for a walk***
Promenades nocturnes - ***night walks***
Doux - ***pleasant***
Clair – ***bright/clear***

Arrivés au parc, les jeunes amis discutent **en marchant**. Sandrine parle encore du film:

"Je ne pensais pas que tu aimais les films romantiques! En général, les garçons ne sont pas très romantiques.

- Ce n'est pas mon cas. Je suis très romantique **comme gars**. En fait, même les autres garçons le sont aussi, mais ils ne le montrent pas **forcément.**
- Je crois que tu as raison. Il faut vraiment **côtoyer** un garçon pour bien le connaître . Un film comme "Le Temps d'un automne" est un **excellent moyen** pour découvrir ce genre de

choses. L'affection qui **naît** entre les personnages est si forte. Il faut dire que même à la lecture du r**oman** on **ressent ça**. De plus, la distribution est très bien faite. Ils ont choisi de super bons comédiens.
Oui et l'histoire nous montre à quel point la vie est précieuse. Tu ne trouves pas?
Oui je trouve aussi. La vie **passe** assez vite."

En marchant - ***while walking***
Comme gars - ***for a guy***
Forcément - ***necessarily***
Côtoyer - ***to mix with***
Excellent moyen - ***great way***
Naît (naître) - ***emerges (to emerge; lit: to be born)***
Roman - ***novel***
Ressent ça (ressentir) - ***feels it (to feel)***
A quel point - ***how much***
Passé - ***goes by***

En entendant ces mots Robin pense que c'est le bon moment pour lui. Il se dit qu'il peut enfin lui avouer ses sentiments. **Prenant son courage à deux mains**, Robin se lance:

Sandrine, j'ai quelque chose à t'avouer."
En entendant - ***upon hearing***
Prenant son courage à deux mains - ***taking his courage in both hands/gathering his courage***

La jeune fille avec un **petit air étonné** se retourne vers Robin et attend d'entendre ce que le jeune homme veut lui dire. Robin reprend:

"On se connaît depuis un certain temps maintenant. Je ne te **cacherais** pas que je ressens plus que de l'amitié pour toi. Tu es une fille sympa, **sûre de toi** et tellement adorable. Ton influence sur moi est magique, personne n'a jamais su **me faire sortir de ma coquille** comme toi. Je suis amoureux de toi Sandrine.

- Eh bien! Je m'attendais à une telle déclaration, **mais pas à tout**

ça. Robin tu es si gentil, je ne pensais pas que je t'inspirais **autant de choses**. Moi aussi je suis amoureuse de toi. J'ai eu des sentiments dès le début, dès que tu es arrivé au lycée. Au moment où tu es entré dans la **salle de cours**, je t'avais tout de suite remarqué et je me suis dit qu'il fallait que je te parle. Je n'ai jamais pu t'avouer mes sentiments, j'espérais que ce soit toi qui le fasses. Ce soir je suis tellement heureuse d'être avec toi. Je t'aime Robin."

Petit air étonné – ***slightly surprised look***
Cacherai - ***will hide***
Sûre de toi - ***self-confident***
Me faire sortir de ma coquille - ***to make me come out of my shell***
Mais pas à tout ça - ***but not all that***
Autant de choses - ***so many things***
Salle de cours - ***classroom***

Sur ces mots, le jeune homme prend l'initiative de l'embrasser Le baiser est très bien accueilli par Sandrine. Les deux amoureux ne tardent pas et Robin **reconduit** Sandrine **chez elle.** Les deux adolescents sont aux anges.

Sur ces mots - ***with these words***
Reconduit chez elle (reconduire quelqu'un chez lui) - ***drives her home*** **(to drive someone home)**

Le weekend se termine et lundi arrive vite. Au lycée, tout le monde est surpris de voir Sandrine et Robin arriver **main dans la main** en cours. Jean court les voir pour les **féliciter**:

"**Alors ça y est**? Vous êtes officiellement ensemble?"
Main dans la main - ***hand in hand***
Féliciter - ***to congratulate***
Alors ça y est? - ***So that's it?***

Sandrine lui **répond avec beaucoup d'assurance** que oui et que en ne les séparera. **La sonnerie** retentit et tout le monde part en ours. La vie reprend son cours **sauf que cette fois** Robin est en ouple avec la belle Sandrine.

épond avec beaucoup d'assurance (répondre) - ***answers with great onfidence (to answer)***
a sonnerie retentit (retentir) - ***the bell rings (to ring)***
auf que cette fois - ***except that this time***

Vocabulary Recap 7:

Sa venue - ***his arrival***
Est devenu - ***has become***
Semblent aller pour le mieux - ***seem to be fine***
Profitant - ***taking advantage of***
Conseils - ***advice***
Sortir avec toi - ***to go out with you***
Amoureux - ***in love***
N'irai pas jusqu'à dire - ***I wouldn't say that***
Fou d'elle - ***crazy about her***
Mignonne - ***cute***
Sympa - ***nice***
Allez, avoue - ***Come on, admit***
L'emmener - ***to take her***
A l'habitude - ***used to***
Certes - ***certainly***
Avouer - ***to confess***
Sentiments - ***feelings***
Vous promener (se promener) - ***to take a walk***
En voilà - ***and here is***
Se poursuit normalement - ***continues as normal/normally***
Fin - ***end***
Cours - ***classes***
Ben - ***well***
Se mettre d'accord - ***to make a decision/to decide***
Je dois y aller - ***I have got to go/I must go***
À plus! - ***see you!***
Aux anges - ***thrilled***
Chez lui - ***at his place***
A en tête - ***has in mind***
Concrètement - ***concretely***
Trouvailles - ***findings***
Ils passent - ***they are showing***
Vedette - ***star***
Écran - ***screen***
L'interprète - ***the performer***
Premier rôle féminin - ***leading actress***

ant mieux alors - ***then all the better***
asse te chercher - ***going to/will pick you up***
ite – ***quickly***
dolescents - ***teenagers***
e plus normalement du monde - ***as usual***
out excité à l'idée - ***all excited about***
enue adéquate - ***appropriate clothing/suitable outfit***
éance d'essayage - ***fitting session***
lasse et décontractée - ***classy and relaxed***
harmante - ***charming***
as de la porte - ***doorstep***
laxonne – ***honks/beeps***
eprendre la route - ***to hit the road again***
rès en beauté - ***very beautiful/stunning***
edémarre - ***restarts***
eaucoup de monde - ***many people***
let - ***puts***
l'aise - ***comfortable/at ease***
lettre à l'aise - ***to put at ease***
vouer ses sentiments - ***to confess his feelings***
rennent place par la suite – ***then they take their places***
rendre place - ***to sit***
'ouvreur - ***the usher***
érifier - ***to check/to verify***
illets - ***tickets***
pectateurs – ***audience/spectators***
ébut de la séance - ***beginning of the session***
Sa belle - ***his beauty***
e n'est pas la peine - ***It is not worth it***
arfait - ***perfect***
Jne adaptation - ***an adaptation***
Je l'ai lu - ***I have read it***
éalisateur - ***director***
Scénariste - ***scriptwriter***
ranchement – ***honestly/frankly***
Époustouflants – ***breathtaking/mind-blowing***
Se complètent - ***complete one another***
La plupart du temps - ***most of the time***

Histoire 7/Story 7: Une soirée au cinéma

Interrompue - ***interrupted***
Passent par dizaines - ***are passing quickly***
Prise par le film - ***taken by the film/concentrated on the film***
Désespérerait - ***would have lost hope***
Fameuse scène - ***famous scene***
Prise d'émotion - ***feeling emotional/moved***
Tout à coup ramené à la réalité - ***suddenly brought back to reality***
Serre la main - ***holds her hand tightly***
Déroulement - ***progress***
Merveilleux - ***wonderful***
J'en serai vraiment ravie - ***I will be so delighted to***
Propices - ***suitable***
Personnages - ***characters***
Figurants - ***extras (for a movie)***
Le maquillage - ***the makeup***
L'éclairage - ***the lighting***
Faire un tour - ***to go for a walk***
Promenades nocturnes - ***night walks***
Doux - ***pleasant***
Clair – ***bright/clear***
En marchant - ***while walking***
Comme gars - ***for a guy***
Forcément - ***necessarily***
Côtoyer - ***to mix with***
Excellent moyen - ***great way***
Naît (naître) - ***emerges (to emerge; lit: to be born)***
Roman - ***novel***
Ressent ça (ressentir) - ***feels it (to feel)***
À quel point - ***how much***
Passé - ***goes by***
En entendant - ***upon hearing***
Prenant son courage à deux mains - ***taking his courage in both hands/gathering his courage***
Petit air étonné – ***slightly surprised look***
Cacherai - ***will hide***
Sûre de toi - ***self-confident***
Me faire sortir de ma coquille - ***to make me come out of my shell***

Mais pas à tout ça - ***but not all that***
Autant de choses - ***so many things***
Salle de cours - ***classroom***
Sur ces mots - ***with these words***
Reconduit chez elle (reconduire quelqu'un chez lui) - ***drives her home (to drive someone home)***
Main dans la main - ***hand in hand***
Féliciter - ***to congratulate***
Alors ça y est? - ***So that's it?***
Répond avec beaucoup d'assurance (répondre) - ***answers with great confidence (to answer)***
La sonnerie retentit (retentir) - ***the bell rings (to ring)***
Sauf que cette fois - ***except that this time***

Practice your writing:

Write a short summary of this story.

Sample:

Sur les conseils de son ami Jean, Robin décide d'inviter Sandrine au cinéma pour lui avouer ce qu'il ressent pour elle. Plus tard dans la journée, Robin propose ça à Sandrine et elle accepte avec joie.

Après une recherche sur internet, c'est "Le Temps d'un automne" qui passera samedi soir au Louxor que Robin choisit. Le lendemain au lycée, il propose ça à Sandrine. Le film étant un de ses préférés, la jeune fille saute de joie. Ils décident d'un rendez-vous et le tour est joué.

La semaine passe vite et le fameux jour est arrivé. Robin prend la voiture de son père et part chercher Sandrine. Arrivé chez elle, la jeune fille, **très en beauté** monte dans la voiture et ils partent au cinéma.

Très en beauté - ***looking very beautiful/stunning***

Arrivés au cinéma, les jeunes amis sont émerveillé**s** par la salle. Robin, lui, est content de voir qu'il n'y a pas beaucoup de monde. Avant le début de la séance, Sandrine et Robin ont le temps de discuter du film. Le film commence et tout le monde s'émerveille, le film est très riche en émotions.

Emerveillés - ***amazed***

Après le film, Robin emmène Sandrine au parc pour s'y promener et se décide à lui **ouvrir son cœur.** Elle partage les mêmes sentiments our lui. Voilà que les deux amoureux sont enfin ensemble.

uvrir son cœur - ***to open his heart (meaning: to confess)***

Le lundi suivant, ils surprennent tout le monde au lycée et annoncent fficiellement qu'ils sont ensemble.

Audio download instructions

- Copy and paste this link into your browser: : talkinfrench.com/download-mp3-7-easy-french-stories/

- Click on the book cover. It will take you to a Dropbox folder containing each individual file. (If you're not familiar with what Dropbox is or how it works, don't panic, it just a storage facility.)

- Click the DOWNLOAD button in the Dropbox folder located in the upper right portion of your screen. A box may pop up asking you to sign in to Dropbox. Simply click, "No thanks, continue to download" under the sign in boxes. (If you have a Dropbox account, you can choose to save it to your own Dropbox so you have access anywhere via the internet.)

- The files you have downloaded will be saved in a .zip file. Note: This is large file. Don't try opening it until your browser tells you that it has completed the download successfully (usually a few minutes on a broadband connection but if your connection is unreliable, it could take 10 to 20 minutes).

- The files will be in your "downloads" folder unless you have changed your settings. Extract them from the folder and save them to your computer or copy to your preferred devices, *et voilà !* You can now listen to the audio anytime, anywhere.

Additional instructions for iOS users

Talk in French products are completely compatible with all iOS devices but due to the limited control of the file system in Apple devices, you'll first need to download the files to your computer. After following the download instructions above you will need to:

Audio download instructions

1. **Import the file in iTunes.** (To make sure the files are copied to your internal library, go to iTunes > Edit>Preferences and click on the Advanced tab. Make sure they get transferred into the correct iTunes folder by checking the destination in the "iTunes Media folder location" box.) Then, in iTunes, select File > Add Folder to Library. Navigate to the folder where you placed the audio files. Then, highlight the folder and click, "Select Folder." Your files will be copied into your iTunes Media Library and will appear in your Music application under the artist, "Talk in French."

2. **Sync your iPad/iPhone with iTunes/iCloud.** You can now sync your device using iTunes or iCloud

3. **Questions?** If you have questions on downloading the book to your iOS device I recommend this YouTube video: https://www.youtube.com/watch?v=a_1VDD9KJhc? (You can skip the over 1 minute and 20 seconds.)

Do you have any problems downloading the audio?

If you have thoroughly reviewed the download instructions and re still having difficulty with the download, please send an email to ontact@talkinfrench.com. I'll do my best to assist you!

hank you. Merci.
rederic

I am here to help!

J'adore my language and culture and would love to share it with you.

Should you have any questions regarding my book, the French anguage and culture, or technical issues, I am happy to answer them. 'ou can contact me via email or through the Talk in French Facebook age.

Email: Frederic@talkinfrench.com
Facebook: facebook.com/talkinfrench

Talkinfrench 2016

Made in the USA
Las Vegas, NV
23 February 2021